Mix, Match, *and* Motivate

107 Activities for Skills and Fitness

Jeff Carpenter, MS
**Olympia School District
Washington**

HUMAN KINETICS

Library of Congress Cataloging-in-Publication Data

Carpenter, Jeff.
    Mix, match, and motivate : 107 activities for skills and fitness /
Jeff Carpenter.
        p. cm.
Includes bibliographical references.
    ISBN 0-7360-4604-6
1. Physical education for children--United States--Handbooks, manuals,
etc. 2. Education, Elementary--Activity programs--United
States--Handbooks, manuals, etc. I. Title.
    GV443.C373 2003
    372.86--dc21

                                2003002286

ISBN: 0-7360-4604-6

Acquisitions Editor: Bonnie Pettifor; **Developmental Editor:** Amy Stahl; **Assistant Editors:** Derek Campbell, Amanda Gunn; **Copyeditor:** NOVA Graphic Services; **Proofreader:** Red Inc.; **Permission Manager:** Dalene Reeder; **Graphic Designer:** Robert Reuther; **Graphic Artist:** Kathleen Boudreau-Fuoss; **Cover Designer:** Andrea Souflée; **Photographer (cover):** Dan Wendt; **Art Manager:** Kelly Hendren; **Illustrator:** Argosy; **Printer:** United Graphics

Printed in the United States of America   10   9   8   7   6   5   4   3   2   1

Human Kinetics
Web site: www.HumanKinetics.com

United States: Human Kinetics
P.O. Box 5076, Champaign, IL 61825-5076
800-747-4457
e-mail: humank@hkusa.com

Canada: Human Kinetics
475 Devonshire Road Unit 100, Windsor, ON N8Y 2L5
800-465-7301 (in Canada only)
e-mail: orders@hkcanada.com

Europe: Human Kinetics
107 Bradford Road, Stanningley, Leeds LS28 6AT, United Kingdom
+44 (0) 113 255 5665
e-mail: hk@hkeurope.com

Australia: Human Kinetics, 57A Price Avenue, Lower Mitcham, South Australia 5062
08 8277 1555
e-mail: liahka@senet.com.au

New Zealand: Human Kinetics
P.O. Box 105-231, Auckland Central
09-523-3462
e-mail: hkp@ihug.co.nz

This book is dedicated
to the many educators
who have helped
children and young adults
develop healthy
and active lifestyles.

Contents

Chapter 1

Design for Success **1**

Chapter 2

Introductory Activities
The First Phase of Activity **13**

Chapter 3

Developmental Fitness Activities
A Focus on Fitness **35**

Chapter 4

The Activity Core
A Developmental Focus on Learning **65**

Chapter 5

It's Time to Close
Motivators to Bring Them Back **125**

Chapter 6

Celebrating Student Success **145**

Activity Finder

Activity Name	Page Number	Age Level	Lesson Component	Core Activity Skills	Health-Related Fitness Component
Aerobic Circuit	59	I	DF		AF, MS, ME
Aerobic Relay	47	I	DF		AF, MS, ME
Alligator Hunter Tag	127	P	CL		AF
Anything Goes	148	P, I	CU		AF, F, MS, ME
Balance Boards and Balance Disks	123	P, I	CO	MB	ME

(continued)

Activity Name	Page Number	Age Level	Lesson Component	Core Activity Skills	Health-Related Fitness Component
Basketball Basics	68	P	CO	TC, VD, MB	
Basketball Basics	69	I	CO	TC, VD, MB	
Basketball Skill Challenges	70	P, I	CO	TC, VD, MB, ST	AF
Basketball Skill Challenges	72	P	CO		
Basketball Skill Challenges	74	I	CO		AF
Beanbag Grab	138	I	CL		AF
Beat the Ball	108	P	CO	TC, MB, SC	AF
Bump and Set Volleyball	99	I	CO	VD, MB, ST, SC	
Can't Steal It Basketball	76	P	CO	TC, VD, MB, ST, SC	AF
Cascading Ball Relay	142	I	CL		
Catch It Basketball	75	P	CO	TC	AF
Challenges for Today	132	P	CL		AF, F, MS, ME
Challenges for Today	142	I	CL		AF, F, MS, ME
Circle Set	97	P	CO	VD, TC	
Circuit Without Stations	61	I	DF		AF, ME
Club Fitness	56	I	DF		AF, F, MS, ME
Fast Pass	23	P, I	I		AF
Fitness Partners	62	I	DF		AF, F, ME
Fitness Relay	52	I	DF		AF
Five-Minute Action	42	P	DF		AF, MS, ME

Activity Name	Page Number	Age Level	Lesson Component	Core Activity Skills	Health-Related Fitness Component
Floor Hockey Basics	111	P	CO	SK, MB	
Floor Hockey Basics	113	I	CO	SK, MB, ST	AF
Floor Hockey Skill Challenges	114	P	CO	SK, MB, ST	
Floor Hockey Skill Challenges	116	I	CO	SK, MB, ST, SC	AF
Floor Hockey Softball	120	I	CO	SK, MB, ST	AF
Four-Ball Newcomb	98	P	CO	TC, MB, SC	
Four-Team Tag	30	I	I		AF
Full-Court Leap Frog	135	I	CL		AF, F, MS, ME
Great Ball Hunt, The	19	P	I		AF
Great Ball Walk, The	135	P, I	CL		ME
Great Circle Chase, The	131	P	CL		AF
Great Race, The	129	P	CL		AF, F, ME
Great Race Across, The	17	P	I		AF, ME
Groups of Animals	126	P	CL		AF, ME
Handoff	34	I	I		AF, MS, ME
Hockey Bandits	117	P	CO	SK, MB, ST	AF
Indoor Action Soccer	88	I	CO	SK, MB, ST, SC	AF
Inside–Outside Fitness	44	P	DF		AF, MS, ME
Interception	32	I	I		AF
Jugglebug	29	I	I		

(continued)

Activity Name	Page Number	Age Level	Lesson Component	Core Activity Skills	Health-Related Fitness Component
Jump the Rivers	128	P	CL		AF, ME
Knock Down	16	P	I		AF
Knock-Down Soccer	86	P	CO	SK, MB, ST	AF
Look At Me	39	P	DF		AF, F, MS, ME
Lucky Dice Roll	46	P, I	DF		AF, MS, ME
Mat Flip	60	I	DF		AF, ME
Meet in the Middle	51	I	DF		AF, ME
Missing Spot, The	44	P	DF		AF
More or Less Tag	24	P, I	I		AF
Move It	134	P, I	CL		
Move That Ball Challenge	26	I	I		AF
Moving Target	18	P	I		
Muscle-Up Aerobics	49	I	DF		AF, MS, ME
Muscle-Up Challenges	32	I	I		MS, ME
My Group–Your Group	37	P	DF		AF, MS, ME
New Ball Hockey	119	I	CO	SK, MB, ST, SC	AF
Numbers Run	22	P	I		AF
One-Shot Basketball	76	I	CO	TC, VD, MB, ST, SC	AF
One-on-One Soccer	90	I	CO	SK, MB, ST	AF
Partner Challenges	41	P	DF		AF, MS, ME

Activity Name	Page Number	Age Level	Lesson Component	Core Activity Skills	Health-Related Fitness Component
Partner Stations	50	I	DF		AF, ME
Partners—Guard Your Cone	31	I	I		AF
Physical Education Challenge	151	I	CU		AF, F, MS, ME
Pogo Sticks	122	P, I	CO	MB, ST	AF, ME
Rock, Paper, Scissors Tag	139	I	CL		AF
Run and Gun Basketball	77	I	CO	TC	AF
Safety Tag	15	P	I		AF
Sit on My Knee Tag	140	I	CL		AF
Skills-R-Us	146	P, I	CU		
Soccer Basics	78	P	CO	SK, MB	
Soccer Basics	80	I	CO	SK, MB	
Soccer Grab	87	P	CO	SK, MB, ST	AF
Soccer Skill Challenges	81	P	CO	SK, MB	
Soccer Skill Challenges	84	I	CO	SK, MB, ST	
Softball Basics	101	P	CO	TC, SK	
Softball Basics	102	I	CO	TC, MB, SK, ST	
Softball Points	109	I	CO	TC, SK, MB, ST	AF
Softball Skill Challenges	103	P	CO	TC, MB, SK	
Softball Skill Challenges	105	I	CO	TC, MB, SK, ST	
Softball Targets	106	P	CO	TC	
Spell and Pass	130	P	CL		

(continued)

Activity Name	Page Number	Age Level	Lesson Component	Core Activity Skills	Health-Related Fitness Component
Spot Challenge	25	I	I		AF, F, MS, ME
Squeeze Play	136	I	CL		
Station Run	20	P	I		AF, MS, ME
Stilts	122	P, I	CO	MB, ST	AF, MS, ME
Team Balloon Volley	141	I	CL		
Team Line Touch	28	I	I		AF
Team Race Hockey	118	P	CO	SK, MB	AF
Three-Person Line Tag	27	I	I		AF
Three-Group Obstacle Course	53	I	DF		AF
Three-Team Softball	110	I	CO		AF
Throw and Run	15	P	I		AF
Trio Tag	137	I	CL		AF
Unicycles	123	P, I	CO	MB, ST, SC	ME
Volleyball Basics	90	P	CO	VD, TC	
Volleyball Basics	92	I	CO	VD, MB	
Volleyball Rotation	100	I	CO	VD, MB, ST, SC	
Volleyball Skill Challenges	93	P	CO	VD, MB	
Volleyball Skill Challenges	95	I	CO	VD, MB, ST	
Walk With the Animals	36	P	DF		AF, MS, ME
What're You Doing?	127	P	CL		AF, F, MS
What're You Doing—Too?	140	I	CL		AF, F, ME

Preface

Every teacher can use a new idea to show children that physical activity can be fun and meaningful, shifting the emphasis away from winning and losing and reinforcing the concepts of skill development and fitness while instilling the desire to actively participate for themselves rather than for others (for example, their teachers or parents). To be successful in providing opportunities for all students to acquire the necessary knowledge and skills leading toward a healthy and active lifestyle, teachers must give their students varied experiences based on individual considerations presented in a variety of instructional settings.

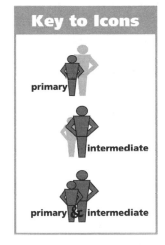

This book centers on the developmental concept of providing activities based on the age and physical capabilities of individual students in a variety of instructional settings. Whereas traditional programs find all students performing the same skill or participating in the same activity, the developmentally centered program approach is progressive in nature and focused on individual student success, creativity, and motivation toward lifelong participation.

Although each chapter in this book provides specific information and activities, it is the combination of information, or activities, from each chapter that will assist in the development and implementation of a comprehensive program with the desired successful student outcomes. Choosing various activities from each chapter also allows the reader to create many different activities for each day and each year, so the students have a variety of activities to participate in.

Within each chapter, activities are listed for both primary and intermediate students. The easy-to-use format allows teachers to create individual lessons for students, or groups of students, using a combination of primary and intermediate activities to meet specific needs. When referencing an activity, teachers will find specific information:

- Age Levels: What grade band—primary or intermediate—should I use this activity at?
- Activity Overview: What is the activity and how does it fit into my lesson?
- Equipment Needed: What do I need to present the activity?
- Preparation: What do I need to do to get ready for the activity?
- Directions: What do I tell the students?
- Hints and Modifications: What can I do to be more effective or to change the activity a bit for the students?

Teachers may also use the activity finder on page vii for an easy reference to the age levels, lesson components, and health-related fitness components aligned with each activity in this book. The activity finder also notes the core activity skills developed by the core activities in chapter 4. These skills include throwing and catching, striking and kicking, volleying and dribbling, movement and balance, skill combinations and technique, and strategies and communication.

All of the activities in this book meet one or more of the following National Standards for Physical Education:*

- National Standard for Physical Education 1: "Demonstrates competency in many movement forms and proficiency in a few movement forms" (NASPE 1995, p. 2).
- National Standard for Physical Education 2: "Applies movement concepts and principles to the learning and development of motor skills" (NASPE 1995, p. 2).
- National Standard for Physical Education 3: "Exhibits a physically active lifestyle" (NASPE 1995, p. 2).
- National Standard for Physical Education 4: "Achieves and maintains a health-enhancing level of physical fitness" (NASPE 1995, p. 3).

Chapter 1 provides straightforward information on guidelines for the successful development and implementation of a developmentally and student-centered program designed for maximum student success. Specific information regarding program philosophy, outcomes, class organization, scheduling, and student safety provide a sound

*Reprinted from *Moving Into the Future: National Standards for Physical Education* (1995) with permission from the National Association for Sport and Physical Education (NASPE), 1900 Association Drive, Reston, VA 20191-1599.

foundation on which to begin formulating programs using the activities found in later chapters.

Chapter 2 provides successful introductory activities designed to be used at the beginning of each class to meet the student's need for immediate activity. These activities also act as a beginning warm-up, preparing the body for more strenuous activity while setting the tone for active participation.

Chapter 3 focuses on developmental fitness activities designed for maximum benefit within the lesson component focusing on physical fitness. The activities presented offer sufficient intensity to develop strength, endurance, and flexibility in a developmental range from basic teacher-led routines to those providing a creative twist to enhance motivation. The activities presented in this chapter are designed to provide 8 to 10 minutes of challenging activity directly related to physical fitness.

Chapter 4 combines skill development and motivational activities. These activities form the teaching core of the instructional program. Activities presented in this chapter range from the beginning, primary level to intense challenges for intermediate-skilled students. Presentation formats include a wide range of lead-up or skill development progressions and active participation games. Activity formats utilize various ideas to facilitate student learning:

- Individual or group activities for both primary and intermediate skill levels, including basic skill development activities, skill challenges, and lead-up games and activities
- Individual task cards designed for both individual and small-group station or learning-area work
- A three-level approach to basic skill development or practice at both primary and intermediate levels (beginning challenges are level one, intermediate challenges are level two, and advanced challenges are level three)
- Individual and group task score cards used to assess and record student progress for each activity and at each level
- Alternative activities using unique equipment (such as unicycles, balance boards, pogo sticks, and stilts) designed to accomplish specific developmental goals at the primary and intermediate levels

Chapter 5 provides activities designed to conclude a lesson successfully. Just as students enter the class with an expectation to move and be successful, the lesson should be concluded with the same philosophy. These activities include simple low-organization, yet focused, games and relays that leave the student with a successful experience and a desire to return for more. Combining the knowledge provided and the desire each teacher has to reach students, a strong alliance can be formed to provide exciting and meaningful experiences for all children.

Chapter 6 provides ideas for school or class activities that celebrate individual and program success. These activities are designed to include parents and community members; they provide an excellent opportunity to demonstrate success. By using these activities and others you may create, the entire school community will recognize the tremendous value of physical education in the development of healthy, active, and successful students.

Physical education provides a unique opportunity for all students to experience success at an individual level. The concepts, ideas, and activities presented here not only will be beneficial but also will spark your imagination to create new activities designed to benefit each student you serve.

Design
for Success

"Healthy People 2010" (Department of Health and Human Services 2000) identifies physical activity as one of our nation's leading health indicators. Prior to the publication of "Healthy People 2010," President Clinton directed the Departments of Education and Health and Human Services in June of 2000 to develop strategies to promote physical activity and fitness. As a result, researchers determined a need to enhance school programs that assist students in the development of knowledge, attitudes, skills, and behaviors to adopt and maintain enjoyable physically active lifestyles. Therefore, enhancing the effort to promote participation in daily physical activity among the school-age population has become a national priority.

To implement programs designed to meet the challenges presented by "Healthy People 2010," school district staff must work to design meaningful programs for all students. This effort requires planned and purposeful curriculum development and instructional programs. No longer can programs be developed and implemented without a comprehensive approach involving critical components. Teachers and administrators must understand the need for quality physical education programs; current program emphasis; national, state, and local outcomes; and program or instructional components of units and lessons.

Those reviewing and designing programs must take each of these components into consideration.

Physical Education— Essential for All Learners

The ever-changing base of educational knowledge combined with the specific needs of today's students have given physical education programs new direction. Gone are the days when physical education was considered a "change of pace" within the school day or an extension of a recreational or athletic program providing games and sports for students. We can attribute evidence of this change to the emerging educational climate of the later 1980s. The following statements represent the changing climate that has provided the new focus for physical education programs (Rankin 1989). Physical education has moved

- from a program that stresses group activities focusing on rules and procedures to one that focuses attention on the students as individuals,
- from learning that takes place only in the classroom to learning that takes place throughout the school and community,
- from content the school and staff believe is important to content the learner will need to achieve lifelong health and success,
- from a program accountable to itself to one that is accountable to the consumer,
- from a program that is an end in itself to one that provides resources and experiences designed for a lifetime,
- from teaching using one learning style to utilization of varied teaching styles to meet varied learning styles, and
- from a curriculum that moves at a uniform pace for all students to one that centers on the individual and his or her rate of progress.

Because of the changing educational climate, educators and students now realize the potential for learning inherent in a planned and purposeful physical education program. Although a developmentally focused and student-centered program maintains traditional objectives, it goes beyond by offering the following:

- Knowledge and movement activities help students develop competencies that are adaptable throughout life. These involve leisure activities, individual or group challenges, goal setting, design of personal health and fitness programs, self-assessment of fitness and activity levels, and adventure or extended learning opportunities using community resources.

- An opportunity to participate in activities designed to be success-oriented provides a sense of personal achievement and positive self-image.
- A stimulating learning environment provides students with the opportunity to analyze, observe, create, and cooperate.
- Knowledge and skill-based experiences help students develop individual plans for a positive and healthy lifestyle.

Outcomes for Success

The following student-centered outcomes for a developmentally focused physical education program serve to complement other educational areas, such as reading and communication skills:

- *Participate actively in physical activities designed to enhance skill and fitness development.* Through a program designed to meet individual needs and abilities, students should be afforded the opportunity to attain an age-appropriate level of health-related physical fitness and sufficient knowledge and skill to participate successfully in a variety of physical activities.

- *Develop movement competency.* The degree of success that people experience in work and recreation is influenced by their ability to execute movement patterns effectively and efficiently. This goal stresses a developmental instructional program that allows students to develop competencies in movement so that they may move with individual success and participate actively with their peers.

- *Develop creativity and communication.* The expression of creativity provides an opportunity to foster an understanding of the individual through movement. Individual or group movement and physical activity enhance verbal and nonverbal communication. In physical education students can learn to express themselves in dance or rhythmic movement and communicate effectively as part of a group working to achieve a goal.

- *Develop a sense of self-understanding and acceptance of self and others.* A developmental program emphasizes the individual. Students work at their own levels, achieving success and avoiding extended periods of frustration. Through the implementation of a planned program of activities focused on the individual, students tend to be more successful and progress and gain personal satisfaction from their participation.

For a program to accomplish these outcomes, the activities presented must serve as vehicles for successful accomplishment and combine with additional planned learning experiences that guide students toward the attainment of the outcomes.

Building the Program

Traditional program development has focused on progressions leading to the students' skillful participation in specific activities such as soccer, football, and basketball. Although the student-centered developmental program also leads to skillful participation in various activities, in this program each component strand—or major instructional element—serves to enhance the movement capacity and fitness level of individual students.

Component Strands

When designing quality instructional programs that deal effectively with the whole child, select activities based on their contributions toward one or more major instructional elements or strands. Every well-structured and comprehensive program should comprise units and activities in the five major component strands. Only when all strands are included in a program can it be considered comprehensive in nature, presenting the breadth and depth of knowledge and activity necessary to prepare students to develop healthy and active lifestyle patterns. The following five component strands represent the foundation for the development and implementation of a comprehensive program that will meet the needs of all students.

1. *Fundamental movement.* Fundamental movement provides a base for complex movement patterns and includes the following areas:
   - Locomotor (jump, skip, slide, gallop, walk, run, leap)
   - Nonlocomotor (push–pull, swing, sway, twist, turn)
   - Hand–eye (throw, catch, strike)
   - Foot–eye (kick, trap)
   - Balance (static: support while in one place; dynamic: balance while moving)

- Spatial and tactile awareness (body awareness: relationships such as high and low; body supports, curl, stretch, shapes, twist–turn)
- Directionality (where can the body move: forward–backward, upward–downward, sideways; high, medium, low; patterns or pathways)
- Laterality (how the body moves: right side–left side or crossing the body center line)

The strand also includes activities that utilize equipment to help students practice a variety of manipulative skills, including throwing, kicking, striking, catching, trapping, balancing, twirling, and turning.

2. *Lead-up sports skills:* The purpose of lead-up sports is to integrate individual skills and movement competencies into individual, dual, and group activities that progressively lead to student participation in full activities at the middle level and beyond.

3. *Leisure-time activities:* This strand includes leisure activities (including racket sports, golf, cycling, climbing, and bowling) in which students can participate individually, in pairs, or in groups. These activities provide opportunities for students to meet their physical and emotional needs by developing the abilities, skills, concepts, and appreciation they need to enjoy a variety of activities throughout life.

4. *Rhythm and dance:* Rhythmic activities can increase fitness, provide cultural awareness, and develop social skills by stimulating interest in and enjoyment of movement. Rhythmics supplement movement strand activities by using a musical beat to enhance fluency. The consistency of the beat also provides students with an opportunity to hear and feel rhythm patterns while moving.

5. *Health-related physical fitness:* Health-related physical fitness consists of aerobic fitness, flexibility, muscular strength and endurance, and body composition. The physical fitness strand provides insights into body systems and functions and how movement and exercise affect them. Physical fitness promotes optimum body function, increased energy and performance in daily activities, and reduction of stress; it aids in postponing and reducing the physical deterioration that accompanies aging. Instructors should integrate this strand into each component strand and maintain time in various lessons to present specific knowledge and activities related solely to the development and maintenance of health-related fitness.

Table 1.1

Percentages of Instructional Time for Each Component Strand

	GRADE LEVELS						
Component strands	**K**	**1**	**2**	**3**	**4**	**5**	**6**
Fundamental movements	65	50	40	25	25	10	5
Lead-up sports skills	0	0	10	20	30	35	40
Leisure time activities	0	5	5	15	15	25	25
Rhythm and dance	30	25	25	20	10	5	5
Health-related physical fitness	5	20	20	20	20	25	25

The next step in developing a program is to examine each component strand and give an appropriate percentage of instructional time for each at various grade levels (see table 1.1).

Lesson Components

After examining the program component strands and the percentage of time to be allotted to each, instructors can develop lessons that provide developmental sequences of instruction. The next four chapters of this book discuss the four components of each lesson: introductory activities, developmental fitness activities, core activities, and closing activities. Each lesson component is designed to keep students actively engaged and successful while they are learning at progressively higher levels. The following tips provide an outline for successful class organization using the four components of each lesson.

Introductory Activities

Students come to physical education classes mentally prepared for activity. Therefore, instructors must establish the tone of the lesson as soon as the students enter the gym by providing a five-minute "quick-hitting" activity. Although you must complete basic administrative and managerial tasks at that time, you can get students moving in several ways as they enter the classroom or gymnasium:

- Preteach low-organization or self-directed activities and have students engage in activity as soon as they enter the facility.

- Arrange pretaught challenge stations around the perimeter of the facility and have students go to a station and attempt a challenge.
- Arrange skill review stations around the perimeter of the facility and have the students practice a previously taught skill.

Developmental Fitness Activities

Make enhancement of physical fitness a basic part of each lesson component. The developmental fitness activities lesson component provides an opportunity to focus on activities that increase student interest and motivation while they provide a variety of challenging ways to enhance physical fitness levels. Vary the activities presented—some should emphasize total body fitness and others should emphasize specific components of health-related fitness or a combination of motor skills and fitness components. Here are some ways in which you can do this:

- Present activities for a period of time rather than assign a specific number of repetitions.
- Increase intensity over a period of time rather than set a predetermined level.
- Design activities that allow for a range of student abilities so that all can experience the benefits of exercise and success.

Core Activities

The core activities component is designed to provide necessary time for instruction and directed practice for the development and enhancement of specific targeted skills. During this time, students work on developing knowledge and skills in the fundamental movement, lead-up sports skill, leisure-time activity, and rhythm and dance component strands. In this component, present only those activities that are developmentally based and progressive in nature. Base each skill on a previously taught, and learned, skill. Consider several concepts:

- Determine the exit goal for each grade level and skill.
- Develop a sequential curriculum based on achieving the existing outcomes for each grade level and activity.
- Make an assessment plan to determine whether students achieved the outcomes.

Closing Activities

Each lesson needs to end on a fun and active note. You have challenged the students during the fitness and core components, and they now are ready to relax and have fun and again experience success. When instructors provide this opportunity, students leave the class feeling "upbeat" and will look forward to the next class. In providing closing activities, follow these simple rules:

- Keep the activity simple.
- Involve all students at the same time.
- Ensure success for all students (i.e., no elimination) and have fun with them.

Finally, make each class period active. As the lesson moves from one component to the next, keep the transition time fast-paced and smooth. If, during the lesson core, students become frustrated or the tempo slows, stop and have them do a simple challenge (e.g., "Can you do a 'Frog-Stand' for 10 seconds?" or "Everyone crab walk around your area." By providing a change in the tempo and activity, you keep students active and involved.

Instructional Considerations

One of the major differences between the traditional approach to instruction and today's teaching practices is that the latter are developmental and student-centered in nature. The teacher spends time discerning what students need to know and want to participate in, then compare this information with what happens during traditional teacher-centered programs. This student-centered approach is designed to provide each student with maximal involvement in activities.

Teaching Styles

Different teaching styles are also incorporated into today's practices; these range from teacher-led to student-directed and individualized instruction. If you want to personalize and give consideration to the cognitive and affective domains during class, you must make problem solving a vital component. The problem-solving method has become an important instructional approach within the fundamental movement strand as well as within other strands for instructors who need to deal with teamwork and strategies. This method involves direction by the teacher and leads students toward specific goals or solutions to a problem. Teachers might pose a question such as, "Can you find the best way to bounce a ball to your partner? Try one-hand and two-hand throws and high and low bounces."

You can employ other instructional techniques, including direct instruction, in which you provide all direction to the pattern and allow little variation. This method is best used when the focus is on a selected or specific activity skill or technique. An example of this approach might be, "Dribble the ball down the court between the cones and back using the right hand." The competency-based approach focuses on self-directed learning and involves specified tasks. Tasks may be part of the general activity goal or of individual goals. As the students practice various skills, they self-evaluate their progress and move toward the established end goal. In the competency-based approach, as well as in a station approach to direct instruction, the use of progressive-level task cards and student journals and logs is important. Progressive-level task cards provide students with a specific list of tasks designed to lead toward a stated goal. For example, the goal may be to perform a basketball chest pass. Here are the tasks that would lead to this stated goal:

- Level 1: Standing 5 feet (1.5 meters) from a wall, complete 10 chest passes. Then repeat at 10 feet (3 meters) from the wall.
- Level 2: Standing 5 feet (1.5 meters) from a wall, complete 10 chest passes into a 24-inch (62-centimeter) hula hoop taped to the wall. Then repeat at 10 feet (3 meters) from the wall.
- Level 3: Place a 12-inch (31-centimeter) target on the wall, 4 feet (1.2 meters) off the ground. Stand 5 feet (1.5 meters) away at a 45-degree angle to the target. Pass the ball into the target, move to the other side, and catch it before the ball bounces. Repeat from the other side. Repeat from both sides 10 times without a miss.

Students can make use of student journals and logs to maintain records of their progress toward a stated goal. Information recorded includes activities done both in class and outside of school. Student journals serve as both an individualized record of progress and as an instructional tool for the development of personal responsibility for a healthy, active lifestyle.

Time

Time is always a big factor in class activities. Therefore, when planning each lesson, allocate time so that students can perform skills at developmentally appropriate levels. This way, students learn not only the what, why, and how of the activity itself but also how each activity promotes the development and maintenance of a healthy and active lifestyle.

Guidelines for Safe Participation

Student safety is a major consideration for all school programs. Instructors and administrators promote safety in physical education through careful planning and implementation that emphasizes the needs and abilities of students. Quality instructional practices, careful supervision, appropriate equipment, and facilities that are maintained in a safe and usable condition must be priorities. In considering the safety of students, review the following important points:

- Activities should take place only after you have provided planned instruction.
- Check to see that students understand the instruction and are ready, willing, and able to begin practice and active participation.
- Students should progress at their own pace while you encourage active participation.
- Always make students aware of safety procedures and precautions before participation and check that they know them.
- When grouping students, arrange them in groups of like size and ability.
- Keep all movement patterns away from equipment in use and other student activity.
- Place mats under all apparatus that involve activities taking place above the ground.
- Always be aware of all student activity and be in a position to provide appropriate supervision and to respond appropriately to any situation.

If an injury occurs, take care to provide appropriate response and treatment as determined by local school policy and procedure. Each teacher is responsible for maintaining appropriate records of all situations and maintaining current knowledge of emergency procedures and emergency-care techniques.

In summary, educators, parents, and students are now realizing that the relationship between mind and body is necessary for the development of a healthy lifestyle. To educate children through physical activity, provide a learning environment that stimulates students to think and to become aware of their full mind and body potential. Students need the opportunity to explore, experiment, create, and select physical activities suitable for their needs. Students also need to have the opportunity to refine and successfully perform skills through appropriate practice. These concepts may mean de-emphasizing competitive situations and eliminating frustration leading to student failure and the potential for eliminating physical activity from their lives.

Always keep the long-stated goal of physical education in the forefront when planning and implementing programs: Students will develop the necessary knowledge and skills leading to the implementation of a healthy lifestyle now and in the future.

Introductory Activities

The First Phase of Activity

Introductory activity at the beginning of the lesson serves two purposes. First, it satisfies the student's drive for immediate activity. When students come to physical education, they are mentally prepared for activity. If the initial portion of the lesson involves inactivity, students experience a mental "let-down" and must again be motivated toward activity. Second, the introductory activity acts as a basic warm-up, preparing students for more strenuous activity. Although students come mentally prepared for activity, their bodies are not ready. Therefore, begin activity with slow, steady movement, increasing to more vigorous movements. When students begin moving in a progressive manner, from slow and steady to more vigorous, their bodies become prepared for the next lesson component, dealing specifically with fitness development. Choose the introductory activity carefully; do not begin at a high level. You will want to prepare students for more intense activity.

Activities presented in this lesson component stress continuous movement that may be coupled with changes in the type, direction, and sequences of the movement. In general, they set a movement-oriented and active tone for the lesson. Include activities such as "free" running, combined with changes in direction and pattern; bending, shaking, and stretching activities using a full range of movements; combinations of movement patterns with manipulative skills, such as tossing and catching beanbags while walking or jogging with a partner; and familiar running and tag games.

Getting Off to an Active Start

Introductory activities for primary students can range from free running or other locomotor movements and bending, shaking, and stretching activities to partner activities involving mimicry or movement with, over, or under partners. At the intermediate grades, introductory activities take on a more organized format, making use of basic manipulative skills, relays, and personal or group challenges.

To ensure success, teach students at all levels appropriate rules and procedures, and give them the responsibility to manage themselves within that structure. Teach the various activities and organizational patterns presented during the class introduction before asking students to participate.

One successful strategy for organization and management of activity is to teach a signal for attention. You need to establish this signal at the beginning of the year and use it consistently throughout the year. Teachers use many techniques to gain attention, such as blowing a whistle, stopping music, and clapping hands. Regardless of the method you use, you must teach students what to do when you give the signal. If you use high rates of positive individual and class feedback, students will learn to respond quickly and appropriately.

Introductory Activities

The activities in this chapter are designed to get students moving, challenge their abilities, and set a tone for active participation and individual success.

THROW AND RUN

Overview

This is a large-group activity that combines throwing and running in a fast-paced and fun format.

Equipment

- One small ball or beanbag for each student

Preparation

- Have students form a line at one end of the gym or playing field.
- Give each student an object to throw.

Directions

On the "go" signal, students begin throwing their object toward the opposite end line. After their first throw, all wait until everyone has thrown; then they run to their object, pick it up, and get ready to throw again. They repeat the throwing and running rotation until they reach the opposite end line.

Hints and Modifications

- Rather than have students wait for the throwing signal after their first throw, have them run to their object immediately, pick it up, and throw again.
- If enough beanbags are available, use them indoors and use balls outdoors.

SAFETY TAG

Overview

This is a fun tag game involving various locomotor movements and agility.

Equipment

- 4 Nerf™ or foam balls
- 10 cone markers

Preparation

- Place cone markers randomly around the gym.
- Select four students to be "it," and give each a ball.

Directions

Students begin moving around the gym. The "its" attempt to tag them lightly on the shoulder with the Nerf or foam ball they are holding. If a student is tagged, he goes to the side and performs a selected movement (for example, jumping jacks or hopping over a line); when the movement activity is completed, they rejoin the game.

Students are "safe" and cannot be tagged if they are touching a cone. However, they may only stay in contact with the cone for 5 seconds and may not touch that cone again until they have gone to another cone or have been tagged. After 30 to 45 seconds, select four different students to be "it."

Hints and Modifications

Change locomotor activities on a regular basis.

KNOCK DOWN

Overview

This is a fast-moving team game that challenges students to move quickly while performing specific tasks.

Equipment

- One cone marker or plastic bowling pin for every other student

Preparation

- Place cone markers or bowling pins randomly around the gym area.
- Divide the class into two teams.

Directions

Designate one team as the "knocker-downers" and the other team as the "picker-uppers." On the "go" signal, the knocker-downers move quickly around the room, knocking down cones or pins with their hands. At the same time, the picker-uppers move around, picking up the cones and pins. After 30 to 45 seconds, switch the students' assignments.

Hints and Modifications

- Caution students to *lightly* knock over the cones or pins and to look before they run to the next object.

- Count the number of cones and pins standing at the end of each segment and see which team of picker-uppers has done the best job.

THE GREAT RACE ACROSS

Overview

This is a relay activity involving various movement activities.

Equipment

- One folding mat (4 feet × 8 feet [1.2 meters × 2.4 meters] or 5 feet × 10 feet [1.5 meters × 3 meters]) for each group of five to six students

Preparation

- Place unfolded mats about 6 feet (1.8 meters) apart along one end line of the gym.
- Divide students into equal teams and assign each to a mat.

Directions

Teams form a line at the end of each mat. On the "go" signal, the first student performs the designated movement down the mat. When she reaches the opposite end, she stands and raises her hand, signaling the next person to go. After all students have reached the end, they begin a return trip using the same movement. After all team members have finished, they sit in line. Here are several examples of movements:

- Animal walks: crab, seal, bear, and rabbit
- Rolling: log roll and forward roll
- Challenges: knee walk, wicket walk, and ball hop. To do the wicket walk, squat like a catcher in baseball, reach around behind your knees, and grasp your ankles. Stand up as far as possible and walk while holding your ankles.

Hints and Modifications

- Link mats together, making a longer course.
- Have students completing the first leg of the course run to the opposite end of the gym before raising their hand signaling the next person to go.

Crab walk.

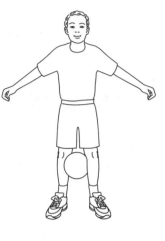

Ball hop.

Wicket walk.

MOVING TARGET

Overview

This is a variation on various target games involving throwing for accuracy at a target.

Equipment

- One small hula hoop, Frisbee™, or medium-sized ball—the "target"
- One tennis ball, beanbag, or other small ball for each student

Preparation

- Divide the class into equal teams, each standing in a line formation at one end of the gym.
- Give the target object to one team.

Directions

The team with the target begins the activity by throwing the target object toward the opposite end of the gym. After the student throws the target object, the first member of the other team throws his ball toward the target; his throw is followed by a throw from the other team. The ball closest to the target earns one point for that team. The rotation continues until all students have had an attempt to throw at the target. The second team throwing the target object starts the next game.

Hints and Modifications

Use a 36-inch (93-centimeter) cage ball as the target object. Students attempt to hit the target and earn one point for each successful hit.

THE GREAT BALL HUNT

Overview

This is a low-organization team activity involving running and agility.

Equipment

- One hula hoop for each team of five to six students
- As many balls and beanbags as are available
- 10 to 15 cone markers

Preparation

- Place the hula hoops approximately 6 feet (1.8 meters) apart on one end line of the gym.

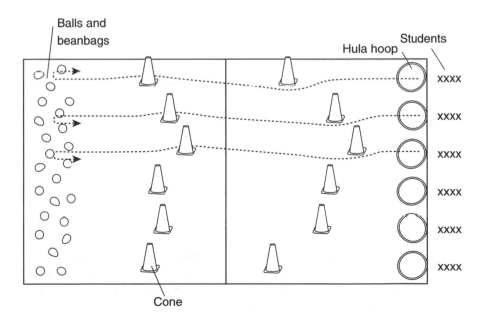

- Place all the balls and beanbags toward the opposite end of the gym.
- Place the cone markers randomly between the hoops and balls.
- Divide students into teams, and have each team form a line behind one hula hoop.

Directions

On the "go" signal, the first student in each group runs to the opposite end (avoiding cones), picks up one ball or beanbag, brings it back, places it in the hoop, and gives the next person a high-five, signaling her to go. The rotation continues until all balls or beanbags are in hoops.

If a student runs into or touches a cone, she must return her ball or beanbag and run back to her hoop empty-handed.

Hints and Modifications

Have the students bring back different types of balls using the appropriate movement technique (e.g., dribble basketballs, dribble soccer balls with feet, toss volleyballs in the air while moving).

STATION RUN

Overview

This is an active station format providing students with the initial concepts of independent station activity.

Equipment

- Varies with the stations selected

Preparation

- Arrange stations around the facility, placing equipment in a box or hoop.
- Divide students into groups according to the stations available.
- Explain the activities at each station.

Directions

Students begin the activity at each station and continue for one to two minutes. After you call time, the students place the equipment back in the box or hoop; then they run one lap, stopping at the next station and waiting for the signal to begin. Here are several sample stations:

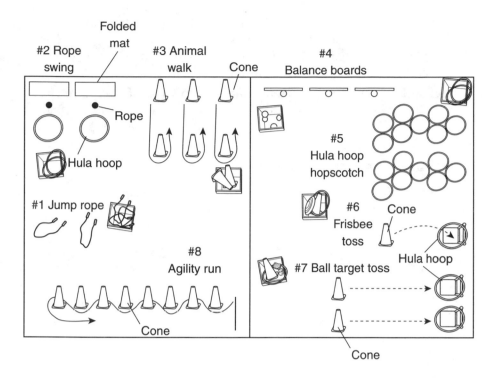

1. Jump rope: Jump rope using individual variations, from basic jumps to advanced movements. Your goal should be to keep moving for the entire time.

2. Rope swing: Standing on a folded mat, hold onto a climbing rope and swing out, let go, and land inside a hula hoop placed on a mat approximately 4 feet (1.2 meters) in front of the rope. Repeat as many times as possible during the time period.

3. Animal walks: Crab, bear, or seal walk and bunny hop between markers placed 15 feet (4.5 meters) apart.

4. Balance boards: Stand and balance on a balance board. After balancing, try bouncing a ball while maintaining balance.

5. Hula hoop hopscotch: Place eight hula hoops in a hopscotch pattern. Students move through the pattern, as in hopscotch, and when reaching the far end, perform an animal walk back to the start.

6. Frisbee toss into a hoop: From 15 feet (4.5 meters) away, toss a Frisbee into a 36-inch (93-centimeter) hula hoop supported on a chair or taped on the wall. Run and get the Frisbee and try again.

7. Ball or beanbag target toss: From 20 feet (6 meters) away, toss a ball or beanbag into a 24-inch (62-centimeter) hula hoop supported on a chair or taped on the wall. After three throws, get the balls or beanbags and return to the start line.

8. Agility run: Run a zigzag pattern down a 30-foot (9-meter) course of cones positioned in a pattern and 3 feet (.9 meter) apart. Return to the start line by skipping, galloping, or crab walking.

Hints and Modifications

Arrange stations according to themes (e.g., balance, jumping, or upper body strength).

NUMBERS RUN

Overview

This is a cooperative movement challenge involving reinforcement of numbers and math concepts.

Equipment

- None

Preparation

- Have students randomly spread out around the gym.

Directions

On the "go" signal, all students begin moving around the gym. After 30 to 45 seconds, call out a number. When you call the number, students have five seconds to arrange themselves into groups sized to correspond with that number (i.e., if the students hear the number "8," they immediately organize themselves into groups of eight). Students not getting into a group within the time limit must do that number of jumping jacks or hops across a line.

Hints and Modifications

- This is a great activity to modify. For specific age groups, call out math problems related to what they are studying in class (e.g., 2 + 5), then students get into groups of 7.
- Begin each round with a different locomotor movement.

FAST PASS

Overview

This is a fast-paced running activity designed for total participation. You can use various locomotor movements.

Equipment

- None

Preparation

- Divide the class into two equal groups, placing one group at each end line.
- Remind students to use safety precautions to avoid collisions while moving—run in a straight line, watch out for others, move under control.

Directions

With groups of students standing at each end line, give the direction to use a specific locomotor movement, and follow with the "go" signal. On the "go" signal, all students move to the opposite end line, using the specified locomotor movement. Upon reaching the other end, students jump in the air, turning 180 degrees, and clap their hands two

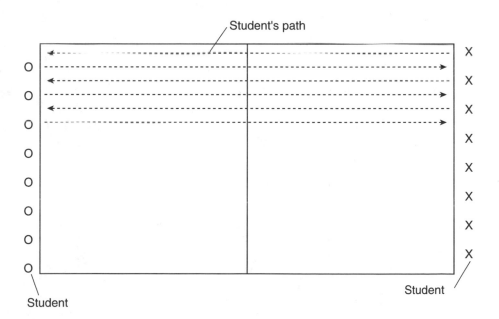

Student's path

Student

Student

times. When all students reach their side, give the direction to "go" again. You can exchange a different locomotor movement for each run or after several runs.

Hints and Modifications

Change the end-line activity on a regular basis—turn and do 15 jumping jacks or turn and do 10 push-ups.

MORE OR LESS TAG

Overview

Using the same poly spot arrangement as in Spot Challenge (see page 25), students choose numbers from 0 to 5 by showing fingers, then add and run.

Equipment

• Poly spot markers

Preparation

• Set poly spot markers across the center line of the gym.
• Students arrange themselves in pairs and stand facing each other with a marker between them.

Directions

As students enter the gym, have them pair up and stand on opposite sides of a poly spot. One side is designated as more, the other less. Students hold one hand behind the back. On the "go" signal, they hold out up to five fingers. If the sum of both partners' fingers is greater than five, the "greater" side turns and runs toward their end line; if the sum is less, the "less" side runs. When the students turn and begin to run, their partners run after them and try to tag them lightly on the shoulder before they get to the end line.

Hints and Modifications

Consider the grade level and math ability of the students, then try subtracting or multiplying. Change the sum depending on the mathematical function you are using.

SPOT CHALLENGE

Overview

Place spots or other markers across the center line of the gym—one spot for every two students. Students line up in pairs on opposite sides of each spot. Give the students various skill and fitness challenges; the students should attempt to meet the challenges.

Equipment

- Poly spot markers, one for every two students
- Beanbags (optional), two for every student

Preparation

- Set poly spot markers across the center line of the gym.
- Place two beanbags (if used) on each side of the spot.

Directions

As students enter the gym, have them get a partner and stand facing each other on opposite sides of a spot. With an odd number of students, a student can participate without a partner. When you give a challenge, both students attempt it, remaining on their side of the spot marker. Here are some sample challenges:

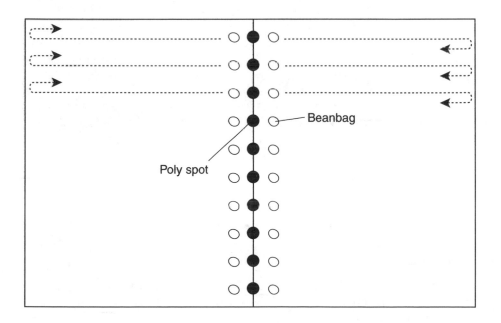

- Run to the end line and back.
- Run to the end line and back, do 15 jumping jacks, and sit down.
- Run to the end line and back twice, do five consecutive 360-degree jump turns, and sit down.
- Perform 25 jumping jacks, run to the end line, and sit down.
- In push-up position, with hands on one side of the line, do 50 quick hand walks back and forth over the line. With the feet remaining in place, move one hand at a time back and forth over a line. Try foot walks from a crab walk position. Use the same concept as the hand walks, but move the feet back and forth over a line with the hands remaining in place.
- With toes touching and knees bent, do 15 curl-ups.
- Run to the end line four times, do 25 jumping jacks, and sit down.

Hand walk.   Foot walk.

Hints and Modifications

Create a challenge between partners using time: How many hand walks can you do in 30 seconds? Who can do 25 jumping jacks and sit down first? Or play add-on: When finished with the task, partners on the left side add one more activity that both partners do. Each partner group may be doing different activities.

MOVE THAT BALL CHALLENGE

Overview

Groups of 10 students each form circles, with tennis or Wiffle™ balls inside the circle. Group members attempt to keep all balls in motion for a specified time.

Equipment

- 13 tennis or Wiffle balls per group

Preparation

- Set groups of 13 tennis or Wiffle balls in various locations around the gym.
- Have groups of 10 students form a large circle around each set of balls.

Directions

Place 13 tennis or Wiffle balls in the center of each group of 10 students. On the "go" signal, players, using their feet, must keep all balls in motions within their circle. When a ball stops, the group calls out, "Stopper." A ball that has stopped cannot be kicked again. Any ball that leaves the perimeter of the circle is considered a stopper and cannot be retrieved. After five stoppers, the team stops playing.

Hints and Modifications

This is an excellent activity to use during a soccer unit. Try using Nerf soccer balls instead of the tennis or Wiffle balls. Remind the class that accuracy of passing is what counts.

THREE-PERSON LINE TAG

Overview

Students are linked together in groups of three. One student lets go and tries to attach to another group, displacing the front runner in that group.

Equipment

- None

Preparation

- Have students arrange themselves in groups of three.
- Remind class of safety precautions—avoid other groups, run under control, and work as a group to move safely.

Directions

In groups of three, students hold onto the waist of the partner in front. On the "go" signal, all groups begin a slow jog. On signal, the last person in each group lets go, trying to attach to the back of another group.

If she succeeds, the front person in that group leaves and attempts to attach to the back of another group.

Hints and Modifications

Stress cooperation and moving as a group. Students may hold onto the shoulders of the person in front of them if that works better for them than holding onto the waist.

TEAM LINE TOUCH

Overview

Groups of students, linked together, cooperate with each other to run from one end of the gym to the other.

Equipment

- None

Preparation

- Arrange students in groups of six at one end line, with everyone in the group facing the same direction.

Directions

In groups of six, students form a line, facing the same direction, holding onto the hips or shoulders of the person in front of them. To begin,

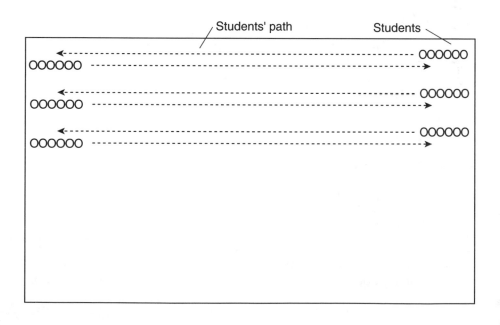

students run to the opposite end line; everyone lets go, turns 180 degrees, takes hold of the person in front of them, and begins to run back to their original line. Groups repeat the pattern, counting the number of lines touched in three minutes.

Hints and Modifications

- Have students move up or back one position after each completed lap—down and back.
- Make the running area larger or smaller (e.g., side to side or center line to end line), depending on the skill and cooperation level of the class.
- Remind students of safety considerations and the need to cooperate and work as a group.

JUGGLEBUG

Overview

Students practice hand–eye coordination, juggling skills, and other movement patterns in a quick, low-organization, and individual challenge task.

Equipment

- One juggling scarf for each student (12-inch × 12-inch [31-centimeter × 31-centimeter] pieces of plastic bags can be used instead of juggling scarves)

Preparation

- Hand out scarves as students enter the gym and have them find a personal space away from others.

Directions

With each student holding a scarf in one hand, give the following challenge tasks:

1. Toss with one hand, clap front and back, and catch. After 10, switch hands. After 10 with each hand, alternate hands tossing and catching.
2. Toss with one hand, move to a front push-up position, stand up, and catch. After 5, switch hands. After 5 with each hand, alternate hands tossing and catching.

3. Standing face to face with a partner, toss with one hand, high-five your partner, and catch. After 10, switch hands. After 10 with each hand, alternate tossing and catching.

4. Toss with one hand, do 5 jumping jacks, and catch. After 10 catches, switch hands. After 10 with each hand, alternate tossing and catching.

5. Toss with 1 hand, lift 1 leg, and catch with the other hand under the raised leg. After 10, switch hands.

6. Toss the scarf to the right side, move to the right, and catch the scarf quickly; repeat. After 15 times, switch hands. After 15 with each hand, alternate sides.

Hints and Modifications

After determining the skill level of your students, add individual challenges (e.g., juggle 2 scarves, clap once before catching, and resume).

FOUR-TEAM TAG

Overview

This is an active tag game involving teamwork and various movement skills.

Equipment

- Timer
- Different-colored pinnies or other identifying markings for four equal teams

Preparation

- Divide the class into four equal groups, giving each group a different identification marker (e.g., pinnies or wrist or arm bands).
- Have students space themselves randomly around the room—not by team.

Directions

On the "go" signal, students begin moving around the gym. After 15 seconds, call out an identifying color of one team and start the timer. Members of that team attempt to tag members of the other teams lightly on the shoulder. When tagged, students go to the sideline. After all players have been tagged, stop the timer. Everyone comes back to the playing area, and the game begins again when you call out a new color.

Hints and Modifications

- Change locomotor movements for each group (e.g., during the first rotation everyone jogs, during the second they skip, the third is a gallop, and the fourth goes back to a jog).
- Remind students that all tags are light touches. You can give the tagging team foam or Nerf balls to hold and tag with—this also can be another identification method.

PARTNERS—GUARD YOUR CONE

Overview

This is a cooperative game involving throwing at a target, guarding, and using teamwork.

Equipment

- One cone or plastic bowling pin for each group of two students
- Five to seven Nerf soccer balls

Preparation

- Randomly place cones or pins around the gym—one cone for each group of two students.
- Have the students get a partner and move to a cone or pin.
- Have each partner group decide which partner is the first thrower; the other partner becomes the first cone or pin guard.

Directions

With partners standing at their cone or pin, give a ball to the first thrower. On the "go" signal, the players with the ball throw it and attempt to hit the cone or pin of another group while their partner guards their pin. While holding a ball, students can take 5 steps before they must throw at a target. When a team's cone or pin is hit, the cone or pin guard must pick it up, run to the sideline, and repair it by doing 15 jumping jacks; then he may return to the game, switching positions of thrower and guard. Students guarding their cone must stand about 12 inches (31 centimeters) away from the cone and may not touch their cone. If the guarding player touches the cone or stands too close, the group must go to the sideline as if their cone was hit.

Hints and Modifications

Caution students to throw at the target and not simply to throw the ball randomly. Remind students to run and get their balls quickly after they throw them, then move toward another cone. This keeps the game moving quickly and adds to the excitement.

INTERCEPTION

Overview

This is an active game reinforcing skills of throwing, catching, guarding, and using teamwork.

Equipment

- Two Nerf footballs or soccer balls
- Identifying pinnies for one team

Preparation

- Divide the class into two equal teams and assign each team one end of the gym to defend.
- Give each team one ball to begin with.

Directions

Explain to the class that this is a modification of keep away. Each team attempts to run and pass the ball down the court and across the opponent's end line. In moving the ball, students may move anywhere on the court. When holding the ball, offensive players may take five steps before passing. If an opponent tags an offensive player who's holding the ball, the offensive player gives up the ball to that student. Defensive players may move anywhere within the court area but must stay an arm's distance from offensive players unless tagging. The defensive team gets the ball if a pass is intercepted or if a player fails to catch a passed ball. A team scores one point when a student carries the ball across the end line or passes it to a teammate standing across the opponent's line.

Hints and Modifications

Stress teamwork and passing to players who are open.

MUSCLE-UP CHALLENGES

Overview

These are fitness challenges that allow students to work on specific areas of fitness while attempting challenging activities.

Equipment

- Printed task cards for each challenge (see form 2.1)

Preparation

- Explain to students that some of the challenges require working cooperatively and the other challenges require working individually.
- Arrange challenge stations around the gym.

Directions

Encourage students to work at their own level and progress from one station to another when they have completed a task. To begin, students go to a station and attempt the challenge. Here are some examples:

- Individual push-up challenges
  > Do modified push-ups (push-ups from the knees).
  > Keep your hands wide.
  > Do hand-clap push-ups (when pushing up, lift hands off the ground and clap).
  > Place hands close together, with fingers and thumbs forming a triangle.
- Partner push-up challenges
  > Hip push-ups: Partners form a 90-degree angle, with one student placing his feet on the hips of the other. The partners work together to do push-ups at the same time.
  > Four-way push-ups: This is the same as the hip push-up, with four students forming a square.

FORM 2.1

Sample Task Card for Individual Push-Up Challenges—Basic Level

- Can you hold yourself in a push-up position while counting to 20?
- Can you support yourself on the right hand and wave your left for 10 seconds? Repeat with the left hand on the ground.
- Can you do 5 knee push-ups?
- Can you lift one leg while holding yourself up with your hands and other foot? Repeat lifting the other leg.

From *Mix, Match, and Motivate: 107 Activities for Skills and Fitness* by Jeff Carpenter, 2003, Champaign, IL: Human Kinetics.

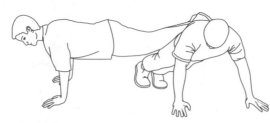

Hip push-up.

Hints and Modifications

- When students have successfully completed all challenges, have them develop others.
- To ensure the safety of all students, partners should place only the top of the foot on the other partner's hips. They should not place weight on partner's lower back or legs.

HANDOFF

Overview

This is a fast-moving cooperative activity involving agility and movement skills.

Equipment

- One Nerf football or soccer ball for each group of two students

Preparation

- Have students each get a partner and a ball.
- Groups move to an open area of the gym.

Description

On the "go" signal, the partner holding the ball begins randomly jogging around the gym; the other partner begins doing jumping jacks. On the "stop" signal, the runners freeze, and their partners jog to them and stop 5 feet away. The partners pass the ball back and forth 15 times, after which the new jogger begins to move around the gym. This rotation continues for 3 or 4 minutes.

Hints and Modifications

Have students do various challenges before switching positions (e.g., pass the ball around their backs 20 times, do 10 partner push-ups, pass the ball under their legs).

Developmental Fitness Activities

A Focus on Fitness

An abundance of evidence shows that the physical fitness levels of school-age children have remained static over the past 20 years (American Medical Association 2002; Centers for Disease Control and Prevention 2002). Educators at all levels continually attempt to develop innovative programs and activities that will enable students to increase both fitness and activity levels. Although time is a limiting factor for physical education classes, you can increase your students' fitness and activity levels with a planned progressive program focused on motivation and challenging activities.

The Challenge of Fitness

Activities that fit students' ability, promote success, and afford maximum opportunities for participation, motivate students. Setting and achieving personal goals rather than pursuing goals set by the teacher also motivate students. Design activities to include elements that guarantee success for each student and preserve the students' dignity and self-worth. In constructing activities, consider the following guidelines:

- Rather than require all students to perform the same number of repetitions, indicate that students should perform exercises for a designated time. In that way, everyone starts and finishes together while working on individual goals.

- Provide a variety of activities using a station format. This allows students to change activities on a regular basis, be challenged, and work to achieve goals for a particular activity.

- Teach students how to set reasonable personal fitness and activity goals, and give them numerous opportunities to work to that level rather than to a predetermined level.

Developmental Fitness Activities

The numerous activities presented in this chapter allow you to vary activities on a daily or weekly basis. Constant variation helps to increase motivation for elementary students. If you include activities that are fun, novel, and challenging, students will look forward to this lesson component and the core activities to follow.

WALK WITH THE ANIMALS

Overview

This low-organization activity uses various animal movements to increase muscular strength, endurance, and flexibility.

Equipment

- Animal cards (see more information about these cards in the "Preparation" section of this activity, which follows).

Preparation

- Teach students how to do various animal walks—they can even make the sounds.
- On brightly colored sheets of paper, write the names of various animals or draw pictures of them and their movements. Place the cards around the gym approximately 10 to 15 feet (3 to 4.5 meters) apart (see form 3.1).

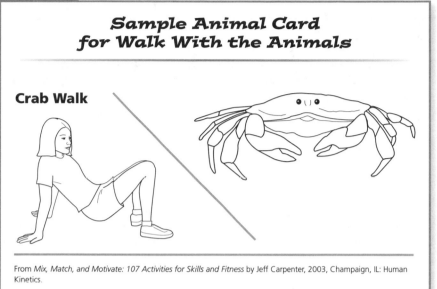

Directions

Have the students move to an open space and get ready to move. On the "go" signal, all students begin a kangaroo jump around the perimeter of the gym. On the next signal, they quickly jog to the nearest card and begin performing that movement toward another card. When reaching the next card, they change the movement to fit that animal. Students keep moving from card to card for 60 seconds. After that time, give the "go" signal again; then students begin to kangaroo jump around the perimeter for 30 seconds.

Hints and Modifications

Sample animal walks: crab (see form 3.1), bear, seal, elephant, dog, horse (gallop), jellyfish, kitten, and rabbit.

MY GROUP–YOUR GROUP

Overview

Groups of students perform general fitness development activities for a specified period. The low-organization and fast-moving routines challenge students through increased motivation and, consequently, activity.

Equipment

- None

Preparation

- After considering the ability and fitness levels of students in each group, determine the type of activity they will do and the time they will spend on it.

Directions

Divide students into three groups and have each group form a line, with each person about an arm's distance apart. Assign each group one activity from each of the following groups:

- Upper-body strength activities
    1. From a push-up position, students lift one hand at a time, wave to another person, and count to 10; repeat with the other arm. Then, students keep both hands on the floor, lift one leg, and shake it while counting to 10; repeat with the other leg.
    2. Students do 5 to 10 knee push-ups, making sure to bend the elbows to a 90-degree angle.
- Aerobic activities
    1. Students jog in place for 30 seconds; the group leader slowly counts to 30.
    2. Students find a line and jump back and forth—feet together—50 times.

Group #1 Upper body strength	Group #2 Aerobic activity	Group #3 Abdominal strength
O O O O O O ⟍ Student O O	O O O O O O O O	O O O O O O O O

- Abdominal strength activities
  1. While lying down with the knees bent and feet flat on the floor, the student lifts his head and shoulders off the ground and waves to another person while counting to 10. Students repeat and wave with the other hand. Students repeat again, waving both hands.
  2. While lying down with the knees bent, feet flat on the floor, and hands on the top of the hips, student lifts his head and shoulders off the ground while sliding his hands toward his knees. He stops when his hands reach the bottom of the knees. Then he slowly slides his hands back down. Repeat 10 times.

After you give the "go" signal, each group should perform its activity for a specified time. At the end of this time, the students jog in place for 30 seconds until you give them another activity within their category. After two activities, give the group an activity from a different category. This rotation continues until each group has done two activities from each category.

Hints and Modifications

Keep the time so that students do each activity for the specified time. Allow for individual modifications based on ability.

LOOK AT ME

Overview

This activity provides a unique approach to exercise and listening skills.

Equipment

- Mats for tip-ups

Preparation

- Have students line up along one sideline of the gym; make sure they are spread out along the line to give them room to move.
- Instruct the class that anytime they hear "Look at me," they should stop and pay attention for instructions. After you give the instructions for an activity, the class responds with "I see" before performing the activity.

Directions

With the students lined up, give the first instruction—"Look at me; I am skipping forward." The students respond with "I see," and they skip forward. When they reach the other side, give the second direction—"Look at me; I am . . ." Sample activities include the following:

- Various locomotor movements
- Animal walks
- Challenges (as follow)

  1. Frog stand: Student squats, like a catcher in baseball, with her elbows inside her knees, pushing out; she places her hands on the floor between her feet. As she slowly leans forward, she lifts her feet off the ground and takes the weight on her hands—while still pushing out on the inside of her knees with her elbows.

  2. Three-point tip-up: This activity should be done on a mat. Instruct the student to use the same technique as in the frog stand, slowly leaning forward, lifting his feet off the ground. However, he should continue to lean forward, placing his forehead on the mat, balancing on his forehead and hands.

  3. Mountain climbers
  4. Bend and twist
  5. Log rolls
  6. Jumping high fives with a partner
  7. Modified push-ups

Three-point tip-up.

Frog stand.

Mountain climbers.

Hints and Modifications

- After the students understand the concept, student leaders give the directions.
- Rather than have the class line up on a sideline, have them spread randomly around the gym.

PARTNER CHALLENGES

Overview

Partner challenges are quick, cooperative, and motivational tasks that build fitness and partnering skills.

Equipment

- None

Preparation

- Have students each get a partner of similar build and find a space away from other groups.

Directions

These activities are designed to be used as quick challenges at the beginning of class or as a "fitness break" during other parts of the lesson. To provide a successful experience for each student, consider individual developmental levels when assigning the challenges.

To begin, give the directions for the first challenge. Allow about one to two minutes for each challenge. Remind students that not everyone will be successful at every challenge and that they may take more practice time if necessary. Sample challenges can include the following:

1. Push-up tag: Partners assume a push-up position, facing each other, about 3 inches (7.6 centimeters) apart. The object is to see how many times the students can lightly touch their partner's hand within a limited time. Remind the students not to pull on the arm or touch anything above the hand.

2. Partner spring: Partners stand facing each other, approximately 1 foot (.3 meter) apart. The object is to push against the partner's hand, trying to make the partner move his feet.

3. Stay close: Partners count off as 1s or 2s and stand approximately two steps apart. On the "go" signal, the number 1 partners begin to jog randomly around the gym while avoiding other

Push-up tag.

groups. Their partners (the number 2s) attempt to mirror the movements, staying within one step. After 15 seconds, say, "Freeze" and see if the number 2 partners are within one step of their partners. Reverse the action, with the number 2 partners now being the leaders.

4. Wall touch: Partners line up on opposite sides of the gym. On the "go" signal, they run to the opposite side, touch the line, and run back. After two minutes, partners get together and add the total lines they touched.

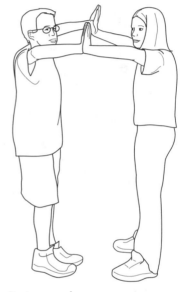

Partner spring.

Hints and Modifications

Have students or groups develop and lead the challenges.

FIVE-MINUTE ACTION

Overview

A quick low-organization fitness motivator for total involvement and activity

Equipment

- None

Preparation

- As the class enters the gym, have the students find a place away from one another and get ready for action.

Directions

On the "go" signal, the students begin the first activity. Move to another location (from a sideline to the center). After 30 seconds of activity, have the students "find" you and begin the second activity. Repeat this rotation 10 times, for a total of 5 minutes. Sample activities can include the following:

1. Jumping jacks
2. Crab kicks
3. Jog in place
4. Mountain climbers (see figure on page 40)
5. Crunches
6. Curl-ups
7. Crab dips: Holding in a crab-walk position, lower the body from an up position to a sitting position.
8. Push-ups
9. Animal walks (see form 3.1 on page 37)
10. Ski jump: Put your feet together and jump from side to side.

Hints and Modifications

Keep the students moving for the entire time; do not give a break between activities.

Crab kick.

THE MISSING SPOT

Overview

This is a new twist with fitness added to an old favorite—musical chairs.

Equipment

- One poly spot or hula hoop for each student

Preparation

- Spread the poly spots around the gym in a random fashion.
- As students enter, have them stand on a spot and get ready to move.

Directions

On the "go" signal, all students move around the gym, without stepping on a spot. While the students are moving, remove one spot. After 30 seconds, give the "stop" signal. When the signal is given, all students must find a spot and balance with one foot. At the same time you give the signal, begin to count from 1. When all but one student has found a spot, stop counting and give the remaining student the extra spot. All students then must do repetitions of a teacher- or student-selected activity corresponding with the number counted while they were finding their spots. Repeat the activity for four or five minutes.

Hints and Modifications

- Change locomotor movements each time—jog, skip, or gallop.
- After the students have experienced the activity, pick up two or three spots each time.

INSIDE–OUTSIDE FITNESS

Overview

Inside–Outside Fitness combines aerobic and muscular strength activities in a fast-moving and challenging activity.

Equipment

- Jump ropes for one-fourth of the class
- Four cone markers
- Corner task cards

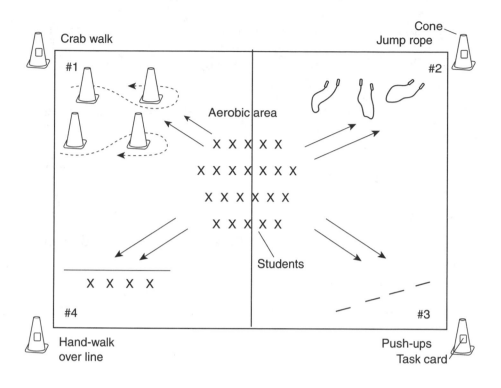

Preparation

- Place one cone marker in each corner of the gym—label 1, 2, 3, and 4—with the corner task card posted on each.
- Divide the class into four groups and assign each to one corner.

Directions

On the "go" signal, have all students run toward the center, keeping space between one another so that they can move. When all students are in the center, give the "stop" signal and begin an aerobic activity—skip, gallop, hop, jog—within the basketball court. After 30 seconds, call out, "Corner 1." Students then go to their corner and begin the activity listed. After 1 minute, they return to the center and perform another aerobic activity for 30 seconds. After they complete the second aerobic activity, students go to the next station, to the left of their first corner. The rotation continues until all groups have done each corner. The following are sample corner activities:

1. Crab walk (see form 3.1 on page 37)
2. Jump rope
3. Modified push-ups: Performed either on the knees or with other variations, depending on ability levels.

4. Hand walk over the line: Executed from a push-up position with the hands placed on a line. Instruct students to move one hand at a time across the line and back (see figure on page 26).

Hints and Modifications

Place more than one activity at each corner. Either have students rotate twice through the circuit or let them choose their own activity.

LUCKY DICE ROLL

Overview

Lucky Dice Roll uses chance to challenge students with physical activity.

Equipment

- One ball for every two students
- One jump rope for each student
- One set of dice for each group
- One task card for each group (See more information in the "Directions" section and see a sample task card in form 3.2.)

Preparation

- Divide students into groups of six, and have each group find an open space.
- Place the appropriate number of balls and jump ropes and one task card at each space.
- Have each group designate one student as the "roller."

FORM 3.2

Sample Task Card for Lucky Dice Roll

Sum of 11

Each group member does 11 push-ups. Use your individual modifications. Remember—keep elbows bent to 90 degrees.

From *Mix, Match, and Motivate: 107 Activities for Skills and Fitness* by Jeff Carpenter, 2003, Champaign, IL: Human Kinetics.

Directions

On the "go" signal, the roller rolls the dice. The group determines the sum of the numbers or the double combination, refers to the task card, and performs the activity listed. After all group members have completed the activity, they sit and the roller rolls the dice again. The activity should be repeated for five to eight minutes. The students can do the following sample task card activities:

- Double 6s: Pass the ball back and forth with your partner 25 times.
- Double 2s: All do 15 curl-ups or crunches.
- Double 1s, 3s, 4s, and 5s: Free pass—roll again.
- Sum of 11: All do 11 push-ups.
- Sum of 10: All do a 10-second handstand or frog stand. (See figure on page 40 for an illustration of the frog stand.)
- Sum of 9: All do 50 Jump rope turns.
- Sum of 8: Standing back-to-back with your partner, pass the ball around each other 15 times in each direction.
- Sum of 7: All do the crab walk 15 feet back from the circle, turn, and come back.
- Sum of 6: All run 1 lap of the gym.
- Sum of 5: All run 2 laps of the gym.

Hints and Modifications

For younger students, use one set of dice for the entire class and have all students perform the same activity.

AEROBIC RELAY

Overview

Aerobic Relay encompasses various fitness and locomotor activities in a challenging relay-type format.

Equipment

- Cone markers
- Task cards (see the "Hints and Modifications" section for task card sample activities)

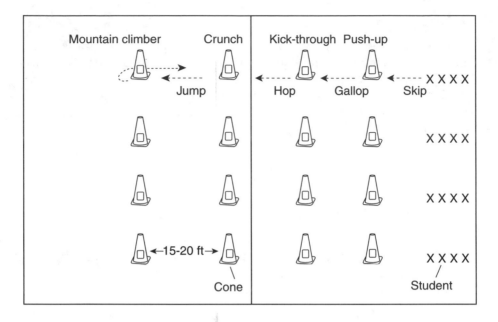

Preparation

- Set cone markers in lines of four, approximately 15 to 20 feet (4.5 to 6 meters) apart. There should be one set of cones for each group of four to six students.
- Place an activity task card on each cone; this card shows the locomotor movement to be used to get to the next cone.
- Have students perform a set number of repetitions rather than complete the activity in a set time.

Directions

When you give the "go" signal, have the first student from each group perform the locomotor movement on the first task card in order to move to the second cone. Upon reaching the second cone, have these students perform the activity listed and move to the third cone. Upon reaching the fourth cone, the students stand and raise their hand, signaling to the next person in line to begin, and then jog to the end of their line. Continue the rotation until each student has had three or four opportunities.

Hints and Modifications

Sample activities include the following:

- To first cone: Skip.
- At first cone: Push-up.

- To second cone: Gallop.
- At second cone: Kick-through. From a push-up position, the student brings his right leg under his body until it touches his left hand. He repeats the movement, bringing his left leg to his right hand. Increase the challenge by asking the student to lift the hand being touched off the ground and balance while touching his foot to his hand.

Kick-through.

- To third cone: Hop.
- At third cone: Crunch.
- To fourth cone: Jump.
- At fourth cone: Treadmill or mountain climbers (see figure on page 40).

Try having two people from each team go each time. Keep one student on each side of the pair's cones.

MUSCLE-UP AEROBICS

Overview

This is an activity that combines aerobics and traditional fitness activities and is designed to motivate while enhancing aerobic fitness and muscular strength.

Equipment

- Jump ropes

Preparation

- Divide the class in half, and have one group stand around the outside of the boundary lines and the other half stand inside.

Directions

After you give the "go" signal, have both groups jog around the gym for approximately two minutes. At the conclusion of this time period, the inside group should begin an exercise set while the outside group continues to jog for the next minute. At the conclusion of the time, the groups switch positions and activities. Continue this rotation until both groups have completed all exercise sets.

Hints and Modifications

Sample exercise sets can include the following activities:

- Jogging—two minutes
- Push-ups—one minute
- Crunches—one minute
- Crab dips—one minute (See description for crab dips in "Five-Minute Action," pages 42 to 43.)
- Crab walk—one minute
- Crab kick—one minute (Holding in a crab-walk position, lift one leg at a time, holding the leg up for the count of 10 before lowering.)
- Cool-down walk—one minute

PARTNER STATIONS

Overview

Partner Stations, quick and a change of pace, combines cooperation and general or thematic fitness activities.

Equipment

- None unless needed for specific stations

Preparation

- Arrange six stations around the periphery of the gym.
- Explain and demonstrate activities at each station.
- Divide students into six groups and assign each a beginning station.

Directions

After giving the "go" signal, have students begin jogging randomly around the gym. The jogging can be done either as a group or individually. After 30 to 45 seconds, give the signal for students to go to the first station, take a partner, and begin the activity. After they spend 1 minute at the station, give the signal to begin jogging, and all students will begin to jog randomly. When you give the signal to go to the next station, the students should move clockwise from their first station. Continue the rotation until the students complete all stations, which can include the following activities:

- Partner curl-up: While sitting with their feet touching, partners curl up together and give a high-five when they meet in a sitting position.

- Over and under push-ups: While one partner is in a push-up position, the other partner crawls under him. The first partner then does a push-up. Repeat, with positions reversed.
- Bicycle: With both partners lying on their backs with their feet in the air and soles touching, they begin a bicycling motion with their legs.
- Ball hop: Each student places a Nerf soccer ball between his knees and hops to a line and back.
- Jump and touch: Each student takes a piece of chalk and jumps up to place a mark on the wall. Students then continue jumping, trying to touch above that line.
- Partner run: Each partner holds one end of a plastic bat between them with their inside hand. On the "go" signal partners begin jogging laps around the gym.

Hints and Modifications

- Use different locomotor movements between stations (e.g., skip, hop, or gallop).
- Have students work with a different partner for each station.

MEET IN THE MIDDLE

Overview

Meet in the Middle, a fast-paced partners activity, has numerous variations to meet individual and class needs.

Equipment

- Poly spots for half of the class

Preparation

- Place poly spots, equal to half the number of students in class, along the center line of the gym.
- Have students get partners and stand opposite one another on each side of a poly spot.
- Once the students are arranged, have them move back to the end line behind them, still aligned with their poly spot and partner.

Directions

To begin, call out a specified exercise or activity. After you give the "go" signal, have students run to their poly spot, greet their partner with a high-five, perform the exercise or activity, and return to their positions at the end line. Repeat the rotation until all exercises and activities have been completed. Here are some samples:

- Do 25 jumping jacks.
- Do 10 push-ups or modified push-ups.
- Do 15 crunches or curl-ups.
- Do a 360-degree jump turn in each direction.
- Do 25 hand walks over the center line (see page 6 for a description and an illustration of hand walks).
- Skip clockwise around the poly spot; repeat counterclockwise.

Hints and Modifications

Use your imagination to create challenging activities. Encourage students to do the same.

FITNESS RELAY

Overview

This is a fun and fast-paced relay-type activity that utilizes various exercises and locomotor activities.

Equipment

- Four cone markers for each group of four students
- One set of task cards for each group (see form 3.3 for sample task cards)

Preparation

- Set cones in lines of four, approximately 20 feet (6 meters) apart.
- Place one task card on each cone.
- Divide the class into groups of four; have each group line up at the end line, close to the first cone in each group of cones.

Directions

After you give the "go" signal, the first student in each group should perform the locomotor movement listed at the start on their way to the first cone. When they reach the first cone, they will perform the activity listed and do the listed locomotor movement to the next cone. After completing the activity at the third cone, they should raise their hand, signaling the next person in line to start, and then continue until reaching the opposite end line. When they reach the end line, they turn

FORM 3.3

Sample Task Card for Fitness Relay

Station 1 (first cone marker)

Do 10 push-ups—use your individual modifications. Do the two-foot jump to the next cone.

to their right and run back to the line and wait for their next turn. Students can perform one of the following sample activities:

- Locomotor movements to the cone
  - > Skip
  - > Two-foot jump
  - > Gallop
  - > Slide
  - > Run
- Station activities at the cones
  - > 10 push-ups: Individual modifications include knee push-ups, triangle push-ups, push-ups with hands wide, push-ups while lifting one leg, and push-ups while elevating both legs on a bench
  - > 10 curl-ups or crunches
  - > 10 treadmills or mountain climbers
  - > 25 jumping jacks

Hints and Modifications

Have two students from each line go at once, with one student standing on each side of the cone.

THREE-GROUP OBSTACLE COURSE

Overview

This is a new twist on traditional obstacle courses, providing numerous fitness challenges in a short period of time.

Equipment

- As needed for your courses—sample courses are shown in the diagram below and on page 55.

Preparation

- Set up three obstacle courses with stations approximately 10 feet (3 meters) apart for each course.
- Demonstrate each course to students.
- Divide students into groups, with each group standing at one course.

Directions

When you give the "go" signal, the first person in each group begins; when he reaches the second obstacle, the next person begins. After each student has gone through the course twice, she rotates to another course.

Hints and Modifications

Designate different locomotor movements to be done at each cone and between stations.

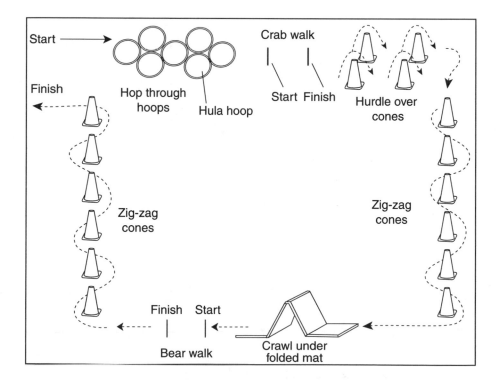

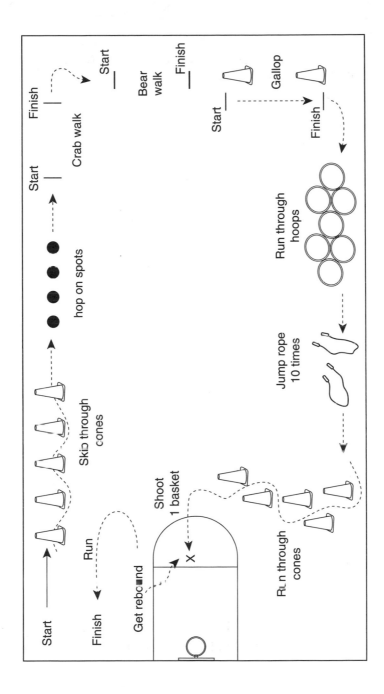

CLUB FITNESS

Overview

Club Fitness, a different type of fitness circuit, involves all students in appropriate challenge and fitness activities.

Equipment

- Six hula hoops
- Six jump ropes
- Six Nerf soccer balls
- Station task cards (see form 3.4)
- Four cone markers

FORM 3.4

Sample Task Card for Club Fitness

Fitness Club 1—Focus on Aerobic Fitness

Choose two activities to complete.

- Treadmill or mountain climbers for 1 minute
- Jump rope for 1 minute
- Ball hop—ball between your knees, hopping between two lines 10 feet (3 meters) apart—for 1 minute
- Jumping jacks: Try different types—ski jump, cancan kicks—for 1 minute

From *Mix, Match, and Motivate: 107 Activities for Skills and Fitness* by Jeff Carpenter, 2003, Champaign, IL: Human Kinetics.

Preparation

- Place one cone marker at each corner of the basketball court; number the cones 1 to 4.
- Place one task card at each corner.
- Have students spread out along each side and end line, between the cones.

Directions

On your "go" signal, all students should begin to jog around the perimeter. After they complete approximately two laps, call out a number

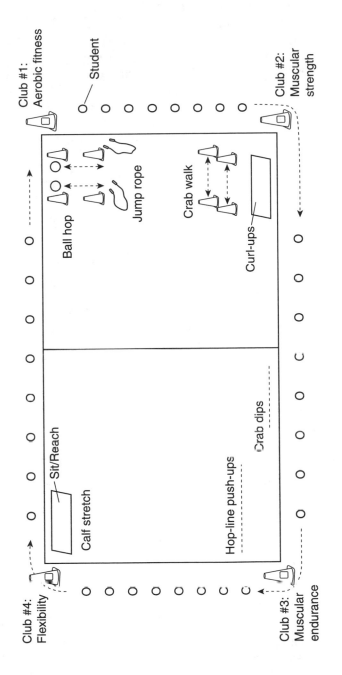

Club #1: Aerobic fitness

Student

Club #2: Muscular strength

Ball hop

Jump rope

Crab walk

Curl-ups

Sit/Reach

Calf stretch

Crab dips

Hop-line push-ups

Club #4: Flexibility

Club #3: Muscular endurance

from 1 to 4. The students closest, or within half of a line's length to that number, keep jogging. The rest of the students go to the closest cone and perform two of the four activities listed. Each activity is performed for one minute (or two minutes of activity for each station). After all students have completed the activities, give the "go" signal, and all students begin jogging. Repeat for approximately five minutes.

The task cards at each cone can include the following activities:

- Club 1: Focus on aerobic fitness
  - Treadmill or mountain climbers (see figure on page 40).
  - Jump rope: Use individual variations
  - Ball hop: With a ball placed between the knees, have students hop from the start line to a marker 10 feet (3 meters) away, turn, and return to the starting marker.
  - Jumping jacks: Tell students to use variations, such as feet together hopping side to side or cancan kicks.
- Club 2: Focus on muscular strength and endurance
  - Curl-ups: The student bends her knees with hands placed on top of the hips. She lifts up the head and shoulders, sliding the hands up the legs until reaching the bottom of the knee; she slides back down.
  - Rowing: Sitting with legs extended, have the students lift and extend the legs while reaching forward with the arms. Students should bend the knees and arms and follow with an extension—as in rowing a boat.
  - Crab walk
  - Crab kick: From a crab-walk position, the student lifts one leg and holds it up to the count of 10, then slowly lowers and repeats with opposite leg.
- Club 3: Focus on muscular strength and endurance
  - Hop-line push-ups: From a push-up position, with hands close to one side of a line, have students lower the body down until the elbows are bent at a 90-degree angle. Students push up quickly, lifting the hands off the ground and moving them to the opposite side of the line. Have students repeat, moving the hands back to their original position.
  - Push-ups: Students should use individual modifications such as knee push-ups, triangle push-ups, and push-ups with hands wide.
  - Crab or bench dips: The student performs either from a crab-walk position with hands on the floor or with hands on a bench. He lowers his body down until elbows are bent to a 90-degree angle.
  - Hand walk over a line: From a push-up position, students should keep feet in place and move one hand across a line and back. Repeat with the other hand.

- Club 4: Focus on flexibility
  - Back-saver sit and reach: Student sits with one leg extended and the other leg bent with the foot even with the knee of the extended leg. He reaches forward and holds the position for 30 seconds. He repeats with the opposite leg forward.
  - V-sit and reach: Have students sit with legs extended and feet approximately shoulder-width apart. They slowly reach forward with hands together, and hold the position for 30 seconds.
  - Side stretch: The student should stand with arms extended overhead and hands together. Keeping arms extended, she bends to the right side, and holds for 30 seconds; then repeats to the other side.
  - Calf stretch: Have students kneel on a mat. They lift one leg, placing one foot even with the knee of the other leg. They lean forward, touching both hands to the floor, and hold for 30 seconds and repeat on opposite side.

Hints and Modifications

Add skill development activities that focus on core activity skills to each station (see chapter 4 for more information on core activity skills). You should keep time for core activity skills at stations. When the stations begin, give the "go" signal. After 1 minute, give a signal, wait 10 seconds, and give the second "go" signal to start the core activity skills. After 1 minute, give a "stop" signal and the signal for all to begin jogging.

AEROBIC CIRCUIT

Overview

This is a fast-moving aerobic activity during which students perform various aerobic tasks and strength-development activities.

Equipment

- One jump rope for each student

Preparation

- Give each student a jump rope and have her find a place on a side or end line.

Directions

After giving the "go" signal, have all students begin jumping rope for 2 minutes. After the 2-minute period has ended, call, "Stop." On the stop signal, have students lay down the ropes and begin to do a strength activity that you have called out. After 30 seconds, call out another aerobic activity. The rotation is continued for approximately 5 minutes. The following is a sample rotation that you can follow:

1. Jump rope
2. Push-ups
3. Jogging
4. Sitting rowing
5. Jumping jacks
6. Curl-ups
7. Jump rope
8. Crab walk
9. Jogging
10. Crab kick
11. Jump rope
12. Push-ups

MAT FLIP

Overview

Mat Flip uses tumbling mats for an aerobic, strength-developing, and fun cooperative team activity.

Equipment

- 4-foot × 8-foot (1.2-meter × 2.4-meter) or 5-foot × 10-foot (1.5-meter × 3-meter) folding tumbling mats (one mat for each group of four or five students)

Preparation

- Place unfolded mats in a line on one sideline of the gym.
- Divide students into groups of four or five per mat; numbers depend on the size of the mat. Students stand at the end of each mat and face the opposite sideline.

Directions

When you give the "go" signal, group members will bend down, pick up the mat, and flip it over, toward the opposite sideline. When the mat lands, the group members will repeat the motion until reaching the opposite sideline.

Mat flip.

Hints and Modifications

- Rather than moving the mat to the opposite sideline, have students flip the mat over after it touches the ground, run over it, and flip it back. Continue this rotation for one minute, counting the number of flips made by each group.
- Using this modification, have students perform animal walks across the mat after it lands on the ground.

CIRCUIT WITHOUT STATIONS

Overview

Circuit Without Stations, an excellent motivator, involves various fitness activities in a fast-paced format.

Equipment

- Jump rope for each student

Preparation

- Have students take a jump rope and find a space away from others.
- Teach students to take their pulse rate (find pulse, count beats for six seconds, and add a "0").

Directions

Before beginning, have the students take their resting pulse rate. On your "go" signal, all students will begin the first activity and continue for 30 to 40 seconds. After the students complete the first activity, give the direction to begin the second. After finishing 4 of the 12 activities, have the students take their pulse rate. They should take their pulse rate again after completing 8 activities and at the conclusion. Ask the students to compare their pulse rates at the different stages and discuss why the changes took place. The following are some sample student activities:

1. Jumping jacks
2. Mountain climbers (See figure on page 40.)
3. Jog in place
4. Curl-ups
5. Jump rope
6. Push-ups
7. Crab walk (See form 3.1 on page 37.)
8. Ski jumps
9. Push-ups
10. Crunches
11. Jump rope
12. Jog around perimeter of the gym

Hints and Modifications

Do not give a break between activities, except when the students take their pulse rates. Each four-minute session should be continuous.

FITNESS PARTNERS

Overview

This activity allows for individuals to perform at their own level while working with partners.

Equipment

• Four cone markers

Preparation

• Place one cone marker on each corner of the basketball court.
• Have students choose a partner and find a space on the sideline or end line of the gym. As they face each other, one partner should stand on each side of the line.

Directions

When you give the "go" signal, the students on the outside of the line begin to run one lap. At the same time, their partner begins to perform a designated exercise. When the first running partner completes her lap, the partners change places and repeat the tasks. After both have completed the first exercise, they again reverse positions and wait for another exercise to be called. Some sample exercises the students can do include the following:

1. Mountain climbers
2. Curl-ups
3. Crab walk
4. Push-ups
5. Jumping jacks
6. Kick-through (See figure on page 49.)

Hints and Modifications

Have large task cards that tell the students what exercises to do posted on each side and at each end of the gym. When both partners have completed the first task, they may then go to the second without waiting for the rest of the class to finish.

The Activity Core

A Developmental Focus on Learning

All students are motivated by a challenge, and it is our task to provide challenges that are developmentally appropriate for each student's ability. Introduce elementary students to and help them refine basic skills that they can use throughout their lives. When you provide appropriate activities that reinforce basic skills in a challenging format, you increase interest as well as the skill level of each individual.

Skill Development and Motivators: Building on Progressions

Skill challenge and lead-up activities presented in this chapter are designed to provide unique experiences that challenge and motivate students. These activities provide variations of basic activity skills at three levels. Students begin at the introductory level and progress through the second and third levels as their abilities develop. When they have completed the levels, they will have refined the basic activity skills and enhanced other areas of importance for good performance (e.g., hand–eye or foot–eye coordination, balance, and agility). After completing the challenge-level tasks, students are ready to participate in lead-up games that will continue skill refinement in an appropriate game format.

This chapter combines activities into three areas: "Basic Skills for Primary" and "Basic Skills for Intermediate," "Skill Challenges for Primary" and "Skill Challenges for Intermediate," and "Lead-Up Games for Primary and Intermediate." When using this format to design lessons, progress through the areas by having students successfully perform the basic skills, then move to the various challenge levels and finally to lead-up games. If you use this format, your students will have developed and demonstrated their ability and self-confidence before participating in appropriate lead-up games.

Planning Toward Success

To ensure the success of all students, develop a progressive instructional plan to implement the "Activity Core." Use instructional themes to help students to see connections between skills and activities. See tables 4.1 and 4.2 for sample themed units that will help students build on established instructional skill progressions.

Table 4.1

Grades K–2 Thematic Units

Unit	Sample activity and equipment	
Balance	• Balance masters • Balance boards • Maze boards • Hippity hops	• Buddy walkers • Foam stilts • Balance disk • Beanbags
Throwing and catching	• Balls—rubber, Wiffle, tennis, foam, yarn, sport-specific • Launch boards • Rings	• Beanbags • Scarves • Foxtails • Koosh balls
Manipulative	• Paddles • Parachute • Jump ropes (individual and partner) • Cage balls	• Hoops • Scoops • Wands • Scooters • Ribbons

Unit	Sample activity and equipment	
Rhythmic	• Lummi sticks • Tinikling or jump bands	• Ribbons
Basic skills	• Soccer (foot–eye) • Basketball (hand–eye) • Softball (hand–eye)	• Volleyball (hand–eye) • Floor hockey (hand–eye)

Note: Some of the suppliers that offer the equipment in this table include GOPHER Sports, 220–24 Avenue NW, Owatonna, MN 55060; Sports Supply Group, P.O. Box 7726, Dallas, TX 75209; FlagHouse, 601 FlagHouse Drive, Hasbrouck Heights, NJ 07604; Greg Larson Sports, P.O. Box 567, Brainerd, MN 56401.

Table 4.2

Grades 3–5 Thematic Units

Unit	Sample activity and equipment	
Balance	• Stilts • Pogo balls • Balance boards • Balance disk • Buddy walkers	• Pogo sticks • Peddle boards • Log rollers • Unicycles • Scooters
Manipulative	• Flower sticks • Disks • Spin jammers • Beanbags • Clubs • Buka balls • Koosh balls • Diablo	• Scarves • Volleybirds • Foxtails • Jump rope • Climbing ropes • Scooters • Individual tug ropes
Leisure activity	• Wall ball, Handball, 4-square (grade 3) • Pickleball (grade 4)	• Tennis (grade 5) • Bowling (grades 3–5) • Golf (grade 5)
Rhythmic	• Dance progressions • Manipulative rhythms (lummi sticks, jump bands, tinikling)	
Dual or team sports	• Soccer (grades 3–5) • Floor Hockey (grades 3–4) • Softball (grades 3–5)	• Basketball (grades 3–5) • Volleyball (grades 4–5) • Football (grade 5)

Note: Some of the suppliers that offer the equipment in this table include GOPHER Sports, 220–24 Avenue NW, Owatonna, MN 55060; Sports Supply Group, P.O. Box 7726, Dallas, TX 75209; FlagHouse, 601 FlagHouse Drive, Hasbrouck Heights, NJ 07604.

Develop an implementation plan that will use the suggested instructional themes. This plan should build on successfully performed skills and demonstrate connections between activities.

Consider the following example of an effective intermediate-grade implementation:

- Instructional unit 1: Balance (a basic for all activity)
- Instructional unit 2: Manipulative (catching, throwing, hand–eye and foot–eye coordination)
- Instructional unit 3: Goal activities (soccer, floor hockey, basketball: Each of these activities presents similar formats, skills, and strategies. The goal and some specifics are different.)
- Instructional unit 4: Net activities (volleyball, pickleball, tennis)
- Instructional unit 5: Striking activities (golf, softball)
- Instructional unit 6: Rhythms

Core Activities

Physical education programs are designed to provide all students with the opportunity to gain knowledge and skills so that they may develop healthy and active lifestyles. The first two components of a daily lesson (introductory activities and developmental activities) focus on meeting the student's psychological need for activity while preparing the body for more vigorous activity and activities designed to highlight elements of health-related fitness. The third lesson component, core activities, focuses on the acquisition of knowledge and skill directly related to participation in individual and group activities. Although activities in this chapter are skill-based, presentations and directed practice should include vigorous physical activity to continue the development of individual fitness levels.

BASKETBALL BASICS

Overview
Students begin working individually on basic ball-handling skills. Place emphasis on dribbling, passing, and catching.

Equipment
- Junior-size basketball or playground ball for each student

Preparation
- Prepare alternative situations for students having difficulty catching (e.g., Nerf soccer balls or fluff balls)

Directions

Give each student a ball and have the students spread out through-out the gym. When all are in place, ask them to perform the following tasks:

1. Bounce the ball and catch.
2. Bounce the ball with two hands while staying in one place.
3. Bounce the ball three times using one hand, then try the other hand while staying in one place.
4. Bounce the ball with one hand while moving slowly around the gym.
5. Pass the ball to a partner standing 3 feet (.9 meter) away. Start with underhand tossing; move to chest passing and then bounce passing.

Hints and Modifications

If a student is having difficulty in accomplishing one of the tasks, take note; before having them move from the "Basic Challenge" level, work with them on an individual or small-group basis. Usually, with about five minutes of specialized work, they will be able to move on to the next level.

BASKETBALL BASICS

Overview

Students enhance their basic basketball skills while learning the new skills of shooting and defense.

Equipment

- One basketball or playground ball for each student
- Task cards listing the specific activities to be accomplished at each learning area
- Task check-off card for each student: These cards are one way to assess a student's successful completion of a task. Examples shown in this chapter illustrate both group and individual models.

Preparation

- After handing out the balls and having students move to an open space, review the basic skills of dribbling and passing.
- Use the tasks shown for primary grades as a review.

Directions

- Passing: With a partner 10 feet (3 meters) away, chest or bounce pass. After catching, partners exchange places and the receiving partner dribbles the ball to the passing position.

- Shooting (set shot): With knees slightly bent, same foot forward as the shooting hand, push the ball upward. Aim at a point approximately 1 inch (2.5 centimeters) over the front edge of the rim or at the marked square on the backboard. Because shooting ability varies with age, form is most important.

- Shooting (lay-up): Starting two steps from the basket and progressively moving backward, students should focus on holding the ball with both hands, then transfer it to the outside hand, reaching toward the backboard and tossing the ball at the backboard square.

- Defense: Keep knees bent and one foot just ahead of the other; one hand should be up and the other down. When moving, take short, shuffling steps. Always stay about one arm's distance from the offensive player and between that person and the basket.

Hints and Modifications

To increase motivation and to ensure successful performances by all students, make individual modifications in the level of difficulty of each task (e.g., lower basket height, stand closer to a partner or wall when passing, begin standing closer rather than moving toward the basket for the lay-up).

BASKETBALL SKILL CHALLENGES

Overview

This activity provides a variety of skill challenges designed to motivate students and gives them various methods to practice skills.

Equipment

- Appropriate balls or equipment for each student
- Task cards for each learning area (see form 4.1)
- Task check-off card for each student (see form 4.2)

Preparation

- Duplicate a task check-off card for each student.

Sample Learning-Area Task Card

Basketball Challenges—Primary Level One

✔ *yes or no for each question.*

- Can you sit and toss a ball—no higher than your head—and catch it 5 times?

  ☐ **Yes** ☐ **No**

- While holding a ball over your head, can you drop it, let it bounce, and catch it? Can you repeat it 5 times?

  ☐ **Yes** ☐ **No**

- While sitting, can you lift your feet off the ground and pass the ball under your legs 5 times in each direction?

  ☐ **Yes** ☐ **No**

Think of what muscles you are exercising.

From *Mix, Match, and Motivate: 107 Activities for Skills and Fitness* by Jeff Carpenter, 2003, Champaign, IL: Human Kinetics.

Sample Class Task Check-Off Card for Basketball Skill Challenges

Tasks	STUDENT ID NUMBER											
	1	2	3	4	5	6	7	8	9	10	11	12
Toss ball overhead and catch 5 times												
Hold ball overhead, drop and catch 5 times												
Sitting—lift feet and pass under legs 5 times												
Bounce ball and catch 5 times												

From *Mix, Match, and Motivate: 107 Activities for Skills and Fitness* by Jeff Carpenter, 2003, Champaign, IL: Human Kinetics.

- Arrange three to six learning areas, depending on class size and abilities of the students—the more students at a level, the more areas that will be needed. Begin with two areas for the first two levels. As students progress, reduce the number of level-one areas and add level-three areas.
- Place task cards at each learning area.

Directions

After you give students a ball, ask them to move to one of the level one stations. Demonstrate each of the challenges to the entire class; then allow time for practice. After four to five minutes of practice, let the students know that you will begin moving around to check their progress. After completing a level, students move individually to the next level station.

Hints and Modifications

If students have difficulty with one task, have them try another, then return later to continue work on the difficult task. Provide individual attention, either directly or by using another student, to assist those having difficulty. As noted previously, four to five minutes of directed individual work tends to move the student forward.

BASKETBALL SKILL CHALLENGES

Level One Tasks

Do the following from a sitting position:

- Toss the ball, no higher than your head, and catch five times.
- Holding the ball over your head, drop it, let it bounce, and catch it; repeat five times.
- Lift your feet off the ground and pass the ball under your legs five times in each direction.

Do the following from a kneeling position:

- Bounce the ball and catch it five times.
- Toss the ball about 12 inches (31 centimeters) over your head and catch it five times.
- Bounce the ball in front and to the side for 30 seconds with your right hand, then repeat with your left.

Do the following from a standing position:

- Toss the ball and catch it, above head height 10 times without missing.

- Bounce and catch the ball 5 times without missing.
- Toss the ball 12 inches (31 centimeters) above your head, clap twice, and catch. Repeat 3 times.
- Toss the ball 12 inches (31 centimeters) above your head, turn a half turn, and catch. Repeat 3 times.
- Roll the ball in a circle around your body 4 times in each direction without losing control.
- Toss the ball against the wall and catch 5 times in a row without missing.

Level Two Tasks

Do the following from a standing position:

- Toss and catch a ball in front of your body 15 times without missing.
- Dribble the ball in place 10 times with each hand without missing.
- Toss-clap and catch the ball 10 times without missing.
- Toss the ball 12 inches (31 centimeters) above your head, turn a half circle, and catch. Repeat 3 times without missing.
- Chest-pass the ball against the wall 5 times in a row.
- Catch a ball being tossed to you from 10 feet (3 meters) away, then toss it back. Repeat 5 times without missing.
- Toss a ball back and forth with a partner 5 times while walking. Keep at least 5 feet (1.5 meters) apart.

Level Three Tasks

Do the following from a standing position:

- Alternate chest and bounce passes back and forth with a partner standing 5 to 6 feet (1.5 to 1.8 meters) away. Repeat 10 times without a miss.
- Dribble the ball forward 20 feet (6 meters) without losing control.
- Toss the ball 12 inches (31 centimeters) above your head, turn a full circle, and catch. Repeat 3 times.
- Dribble in and out of a series of four cones without losing control. Remember to stay close to the cones.
- Repeat the last challenge, changing hands each time you pass a cone.
- Toss the ball back and forth to a partner while both of you are jogging; keep 5 to 6 feet (1.5 to 1.8 meters) apart. Jog for 20 feet (6 meters), turn, and come back to the starting point.

BASKETBALL SKILL CHALLENGES

Level One Tasks

- While sitting in a chair, bounce a ball in a half circle without missing; go a full circle without missing.
- Perform a standing crossover dribble while remaining stationary for 30 seconds.
- While sitting in a chair, bounce a ball halfway around the chair, stop, and reverse directions using the other hand.
- From a push-up position, bounce the ball under, in front of, and to the side of your body for 20 seconds with each hand.
- Dribble through a series of four cones with your right hand, turn, and go back and dribble through the cones to the start line using your left hand. Repeat the activity five times without losing control.
- Do a crossover dribble back and forth between your legs for 30 seconds while stationary.
- Do a crossover dribble back and forth between your legs while moving forward 10 feet (3 meters).

Level Two Tasks

- Quickly pass the ball around your body for 30 seconds without losing control.
- Try passing it around your body for 60 seconds without losing control.
- Do a figure-eight rotation between your legs 10 times in each direction without a miss.
- Toss the ball over your head and catch it behind you 5 times without a miss.
- Bounce the ball between your legs and catch it behind your back 5 times without a miss.
- Do a chest pass at a target 15 feet away; hit the target 5 times without a miss. Repeat from 10 feet (3 meters) away using a bounce pass.
- Do a chest pass at a wall target from a 45-degree angle, quickly move to the other side, catch the ball, and pass it from that side. Continue passing and catching for 30 seconds without a miss.

Level Three Tasks

- Make three of five shots from 6 to 7 feet (1.8 to 2.1 meters) from the basket.
- Make three of five shots from 6 to 7 feet (1.8 to 2.1 meters) from the basket at a 45-degree angle.
- Play a game of Around the World, missing only two shots.
- Make three of five lay-ups from both the right and left side.
- Stand close to the basket, throw the ball against the backboard, catch it, and shoot quickly—make three of five attempts.

CATCH IT BASKETBALL

Overview

Groups of students practice passing, catching, and defensive skills in a fun and challenging format.

Equipment

- One ball for each group of 8 to 12 students

Preparation

- Divide class into 4 groups, each forming a circle.
- Give each group a ball.

Directions

Each group of students forms a large circle, with one person moving to the center. On the "go" signal, the students begin passing the ball from one student to another within the circle. Emphasize quick passes; students should not make passes to a neighboring student. The student in the center attempts to touch or catch the ball as it is being passed. If the ball is touched or caught, the student throwing the ball moves to the center. Also, if a bad pass results in the ball's leaving the circle, the player who threw the ball moves to the center.

Hints and Modifications

If the center players have difficulty in touching the ball, add a second center player. If two players are used in the center, the one touching the ball changes places with the passer. Passes can be limited to a specific type—for example, bounce or chest—to provide specific skill practice in a game format.

CAN'T STEAL IT BASKETBALL

Overview

Students with varying skill levels can be successful at this quick basketball game.

Equipment

- One basketball for each court used

Preparation

- Divide the students into groups of three, with two groups assigned to each playing area.

Directions

The basic rules of basketball apply, except that there are no penalties for double dribbling or traveling if players use fewer than four steps. In addition, players cannot steal a ball from a dribbling player. If a dribbling player loses control of the ball or a pass is intercepted, the opposing team keeps it and goes on offense. If a student intercepts a ball while playing on half court, she must take it past the foul line before starting on offense.

Hints and Modifications

For more highly skilled players or as part of an activity progression, eliminate the ability to double dribble or travel.

ONE-SHOT BASKETBALL

Overview

One-Shot Basketball focuses on defense, quick passing, and shooting during a quick game of three-on-three.

Equipment

- One basketball for each basket used

Preparation

- Divide students into groups according to the number of baskets available.
- Each game uses approximately a half court.

Directions

Students line up on the sideline of each court. The first three players come onto the court as the defense and take positions across the court. The second three become offensive players. On the "go" signal, the offensive players move the ball, passing and dribbling in an attempt to take a shot. The defense tries to intercept a pass or steal the ball.

The offense is allowed one shot. If the offense makes a basket, the defense rotates out, with the offense assuming the defensive position and a new offensive team coming in. If the offense misses a shot or if the ball is stolen by the defense, the offensive team rotates out with a new offense coming in. The defensive team stays in until a shot is made or a foul committed.

Hints and Modifications

When you are using this activity as part of a learning progression, first play it as described, then change it to allow one additional shot by the offense if they get the rebound.

RUN AND GUN BASKETBALL

Overview

Groups of students jog while others practice shooting, both groups earning points for their team.

Equipment

- Two basketballs
- Four cone markers or poly spot markers

Preparation

- Divide the class into four equal groups.
- Assign one group to each end basket and the other groups to a sideline. Give one basketball to each group assigned to a basket.
- Have the groups on each sideline form a single-file line behind the end cone.

Directions

On the "go" signal, the groups assigned to the baskets begin taking shots from various locations around the key. The first player takes one shot, gets the rebound, passes to the next player, and goes to the end

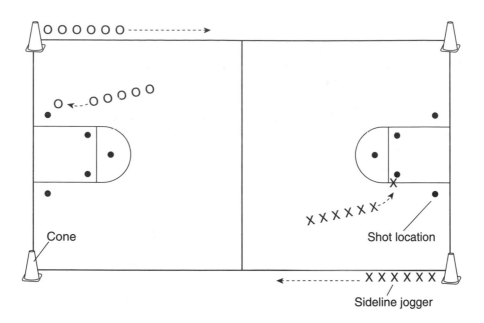

of the line. This rotation continues for four minutes. For each basket made, the team receives one point.

The sideline teams begin jogging, single-file with no passing, down their side to the end cone, around, and back. The team keeps moving for the four-minute time, receiving one point for each completed lap.

At the conclusion of the four-minute time, ask the groups to switch positions and give them another four minutes to shoot and jog. At the conclusion of the second round, add the points for both shooting and jogging to give a total team score.

Hints and Modifications

For students at the beginning levels of fitness or skill, reduce the amount of time spent before rotating to two minutes. Gradually increase back to four minutes as skill and fitness levels increase.

SOCCER BASICS

Overview

Students begin working individually on foot–eye and ball-handling skills. Place emphasis on dribbling, passing, and trapping.

Equipment

- Beanbags
- Empty pint-sized milk cartons for each student
- Nerf soccer balls for each pair of students
- Cone markers

Preparation

- Have students find a personal space; give each one a piece of equipment. Begin kindergarteners with beanbags, first graders with milk cartons, and second graders (in groups of two) with Nerf balls.
- If individual students need alternative learning situations, refer back to lower grade levels. Kindergarten students having difficulty should spend additional time on movement and balancing activities (e.g., balance on one foot and lightly tap the other foot on the ground or move the beanbag between feet while standing still).

Directions for Kindergarteners and First Graders

1. Place one foot on the object, lightly touching it with the toe. Lightly tap five times.
2. Alternate feet lightly, touching with the toe and balancing on the supporting foot.
3. With the object between the feet, lightly kick with the inside of the foot, moving the object from one foot to the other.
4. Using the inside of the foot, move the object around the room. Keep the object within reach at all times.
5. Randomly place cones around the playing area. Have the students move the objects around the area, avoiding other people and cones. On command, stop and change directions.
6. Take a partner and stand approximately 4 feet (1.2 meters) apart; pass the object back and forth.

Directions for Second Graders

1. Use the kindergarteners' and first graders' activities, but replace objects with Nerf balls.
2. Identify the different parts of the foot (inside, outside, toe) that may be used to move the ball. With partners facing each other, one partner passes a Nerf soccer ball to the other using the inside of the foot. Repeat using different parts of the foot.

3. With partners facing each other, one partner moves the ball around the other, keeping as close as possible while maintaining control. After a complete circle in each direction, partners exchange positions.

Hints and Modifications

If students have difficulty when beginning to use a ball, allow them to try it with an alternative piece of equipment (e.g., plastic hockey puck, bean bag, or milk carton), until they have successfully completed the task. If they continue to have difficulty, provide another student who has successfully completed the task to work one-on-one with them.

SOCCER BASICS

Overview

Students progress through a continuum of activities moving into lead-up game situations.

Equipment

- One soccer ball or playground ball for each pair of students

Preparation

- Have students get a partner and a ball and move to an open space; partners—about 6 feet (1.8 meters) apart—should immediately begin passing the ball back and forth.
- When all students have had a chance to warm up, assign each group to a station. These activities presume that students have been taught the skills and have had an opportunity to practice in the primary grades.

Directions

Using a 10-station skill development circuit, students spend about four or five minutes at each.

1. Straight dribble down around the cone and back, keeping control—cones are approximately 20 feet (6 meters) apart.
2. Pass back and forth with a partner 15 feet (4.5 meters) away.
3. Direct shoot toward a goal (to cones 6 feet [1.8 meters] apart) from 15 feet (4.5 meters) away.
4. Weave dribble between a series of cones approximately 5 feet (1.5 meters) apart.

5. Partners move forward and pass the ball back and forth until reaching a cone 25 feet (7.6 meters) away. Turn around and repeat, going in the other direction.

6. Do stationary heel kicks to a partner 10 feet (3 meters) away. To do heel kicks, with the ball behind one foot, swing the foot forward then back, making contact with the ball using the heel.

7. Chest-trap a tossed ball, gain control, and pass back to partner.

8. Punt the ball to partner.

9. Pass back and forth with a partner 10 feet (3 meters) apart, using a different part of the foot for each kick.

Hints and Modifications

Pair students of similar abilities; provide challenges for students who easily master assigned tasks. (For example, assign two groups of two to a 4-foot × 8-foot [1.2-meter × 2.4-meter] mat area—two on each side, sitting with legs in front. Using a beach ball, see how long they can keep it in the air over the mat.) Modifications for students having difficulty include keeping the ball moving without losing control for one minute or successfully passing to a partner from a distance of 5 feet (1.5 meters) continuously for one minute.

SOCCER SKILL CHALLENGES

Overview

This activity provides a variety of individual skill challenges designed to motivate each student.

Equipment

- Nerf and regular soccer balls
- Cone markers
- Task cards for each learning area (see form 4.1 on page 71)
- Task check-off card for each student (see form 4.3)

Preparation

- Arrange equipment at two or three learning areas.
- Duplicate a task check-off card for each student.
- At each learning area, post a task card listing the different tasks to be accomplished. For primary students include a graphic illustrating the activity.

FORM 4.3

Sample Individual Student Task Check-Off Card for Soccer Skill Challenges (Primary)

Student Name: _____ Class: _____

Primary Level One Tasks

✔ *yes or no for each item.*
- Ball Pass: Successfully passes a ball or milk carton (circle object).
  ☐ Yes   ☐ No
- Traps: Successfully drops a ball on knee and traps when it hits the floor.
  ☐ Yes   ☐ No
- Dribbling: Successfully dribbles through a series of 6 cones.
  ☐ Yes   ☐ No

✔ *all that apply*
- Shooting: Successfully kicks a ball into the goal area when
  ☐ standing,
  ☐ moving forward,
  ☐ moving to right, or
  ☐ moving to left.

From *Mix, Match, and Motivate: 107 Activities for Skills and Fitness* by Jeff Carpenter, 2003, Champaign, IL: Human Kinetics.

Directions

After you give students their task check-off cards, have them move to a learning area and begin. As the students practice tasks at each area, walk around and check that students have completed their assigned task. When they complete all tasks at one level, give students a new task check-off card and move them to a different learning area.

Hints and Modifications

If students have difficulty in one learning area, have them try another, then return to the original area. Provide direct individual attention to assist those having difficulty. Students work independently; however, they will need direction and continual reinforcement.

Level One Tasks

Do the following either with a milk carton or soccer ball:

1. Using different parts of the foot, pass the ball into the wall and have it come back to your partner. If using a milk carton, pass between partners.

2. Using a Nerf soccer ball, drop the ball on your knee and have it bounce off and drop to the floor, where it is trapped. Repeat using alternate legs.

3. Dribble a ball or milk carton through a series of six cones approximately 3 feet (.9 meter) apart.

4. Standing 15 feet (4.5 meters) from a goal area marked by cones, take shots while standing still, moving forward, and moving to each side.

Level Two Tasks

1. Standing still, with a partner 10 feet (3 meters) away, pass a ball so that it can be trapped without your partner moving forward or to the side.

2. Trap a ball passed from your partner with the sole of your foot.

3. Dribble the ball, alternating feet, to a cone 30 feet (9 meters) away; circle the cone and return.

4. Using a Nerf soccer ball, toss it to your partner so she can "head" it back.

5. Facing a wall target, use an overhead throw-in at the target from 10 feet (3 meters) away.

Level Three Tasks

1. In a 15-inch × 15-inch (38-centimeter × 38-centimeter) area, keep the ball away from your partner for 15 seconds.

2. Bounce the ball off three different parts of your body. After each bounce let the ball hit the ground, trap it, and begin dribbling.

3. With a partner 10 feet (3 meters) away, pass to the partner and run to her place while she dribbles back to your place. Repeat.

4. Bounce the ball off your knee three times without losing control.

5. Pass accurately to a partner 10 feet (3 meters) away while he is moving to the side.

SOCCER SKILL CHALLENGES

Overview

This activity comprises a variety of skill-developing tasks designed to motivate and provide individual challenges for each student.

Equipment

- Nerf and regular soccer balls
- Cone markers
- Task cards for each learning area (see form 4.1 on page 71)
- Task check-off card for each student (see form 4.4)

Preparation

- Arrange equipment at two or three learning areas.

FORM 4.4

Sample Individual Student Task Check-Off Card for Soccer Skill Challenges (Intermediate)

Student Name: _____ Class: _____

Intermediate Level Two Tasks

✔ *yes or no for each item.*

- Passing: Successfully passes back and forth to a partner while moving?
  ☐ Yes   ☐ No
- Control: Successfully bounces on the knee 4 consecutive times.
  ☐ Yes   ☐ No
- Control: Successfully heads then knees the ball.
  ☐ Yes   ☐ No
- Dribble and Pass: Successfully dribbles, traps, and passes the ball to a partner behind.
  ☐ Yes   ☐ No
- Dribbling: Successfully completes a zigzag course.
  ☐ Yes   ☐ No

From *Mix, Match, and Motivate: 107 Activities for Skills and Fitness* by Jeff Carpenter, 2003, Champaign, IL: Human Kinetics.

- Duplicate a task check-off card for each student.
- At each area, post a task card listing the specific activities to be accomplished (see form 4.3 on page 82).

Directions

After you give students their task check-off cards, have them move to a learning area and begin. As the students practice tasks at each area, walk around and check that students have complete their assigned tasks. When students complete all tasks at one level, give students a new task check-off card and move them to a different learning area.

Hints and Modifications

If students are having difficulty in one learning area, have them try another and then return to the original area. Provide direct individual attention to assist those having difficulty. Students who are working independently, however, need direction and continual reinforcement.

Level One Tasks

Do the following while using a Nerf or regular soccer ball:

1. While moving with a partner, dribble the ball and change directions. Pass the ball to your partner every 10 feet (3 meters).
2. Bounce the ball off different parts of the body, let the ball hit the ground, and dribble it to a cone 15 feet (4.5 meters) away. Pass the ball back to your partner. Repeat.
3. Practice goalkeeping by punching (hitting the ball away), tipping (using the fingers, tip the ball to a teammate), and catching (catching and holding the ball) when a ball is kicked from 15 feet (4.5 meters) away.
4. Staying in a 15-foot × 15-foot (4.5-meter × 4.5-meter) area, play keep away from your partner for 30 seconds. If your partner gets the ball, reverse positions.
5. Punt a ball into 10-foot × 10-foot (3-meter × 3-meter) area 20 feet (6 meters) away.

Level Two Tasks

1. Pass accurately to a partner 10 feet (3 meters) away while you both are moving to a mark 30 feet (9 meters) away.
2. Knee the ball four times in a row without losing control.
3. Toss a ball in the air, head it, knee it, and then catch it.
4. Dribble the ball 15 feet (4.5 meters), trap it, and, using your heel, accurately pass it to your partner standing behind you.

5. Start slowly and dribble while zigzagging between a series of five cones. Turn and go back, trying to go a little faster each time.

Level Three Tasks

1. Contact the ball with your knee, then foot, without letting it hit the ground.
2. Defend a goal—marked by cones 6 feet (1.8 meters) apart—from kicks 15 feet (4.5 meters) away.
3. Standing 3 feet (.9 meter) in front of cones placed 3 feet (.9 meter) apart, kick the ball through the cones, run around them, and trap the ball within 3 feet (.9 meter) of the cones. Repeat.
4. Standing 2 feet (.6 meter) from your partner, head a Nerf soccer ball back and forth.
5. Zigzag dribble between cones toward a goal, without coming to a stop; kick toward the goal.

KNOCK-DOWN SOCCER

Overview

This activity emphasizes the offensive skills of dribbling and controlled shooting as well as defensive and agility skills.

Equipment

- 16 cone markers
- Three or four Nerf soccer balls

Preparation

- Place four cones along each sideline and four up the center line. Assign one student to each cone; the remaining students stand to the side.

Directions

The object of this game is to dribble a ball close to another player's cone and kick the ball into the cone. At the same time, players try to defend their cone from others. If a cone is hit, the player who was assigned to guard that cone is out and the first player waiting in line comes in to take her place. While guarding a cone, players may not use their hands or stand with feet together, thus "blocking" the cone.

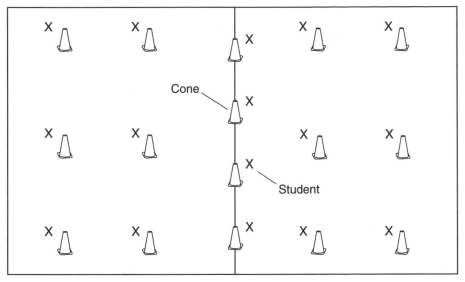

X X X X X X X X X X X

Hints and Modifications

This is a fast-moving game that students enjoy. To keep the game moving, however, players waiting in line must move quickly to go in when a cone is hit. Also, encourage players guarding a cone to dribble balls close to a cone before kicking them—to play offense and "hustle" back on defense.

SOCCER GRAB

Overview

Soccer Grab combines the offensive skills of dribbling and shooting with defensive skills and agility.

Equipment

- One Nerf soccer ball for every two students
- Four cone markers

Preparation

- Place two cone markers, 6 feet (1.8 meters) apart, at each end of the playing area.
- Have players get a partner, get one ball, and stand facing each other across the center line.

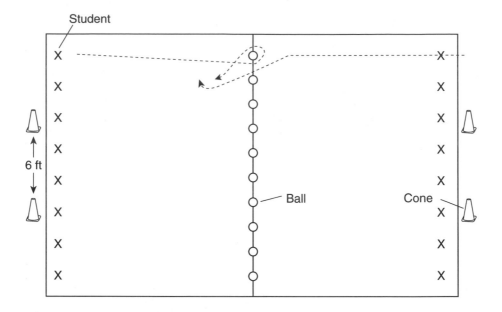

Directions

Have the students place the soccer ball on the center line; each partner should move back to the end line on his side. On the "go" signal, both partners run toward the ball. The first partner reaching the ball gains control and begins to dribble back to her end line. The other player plays defense, trying to steal the ball. If he steals the ball, play is stopped and the ball is returned to the center. If the offensive player maintains control, however, she takes a shot toward the goal; successful shots (passing between the cones) score a point for that team.

Hints and Modifications

1. For younger students, give each pair a number. Call a number; only those students with that number run to the center.
2. Place 2 cone markers approximately 8 to 10 feet (2.4 to 3 meters) from the goal cones. This is the shooting line. No shot may be taken between the center line and the shooting line.

INDOOR ACTION SOCCER

Overview

Students practice basic offensive and defensive skills in a fast-moving indoor game that stresses ball control and passing.

Equipment

- The game is played on a volleyball court. If volleyball and basketball court lines are not available, use 10 cone markers to mark side and end lines of both a basketball and a volleyball court.
- Nerf soccer ball

Preparation

- Divide the class into two teams, each standing on the end line of a basketball court. Have half of each team move onto the volleyball court to become "active" players.

Directions

"Active" players—those within the volleyball court—dribble, pass, and shoot while the goalies defend their goal lines. Those students designated as goalies must stay on the end line. Only active players move on the court; they must stay within the volleyball court, and all shots are taken from within that area. Goalies must stay between the basketball court end line and the back line of the volleyball court.

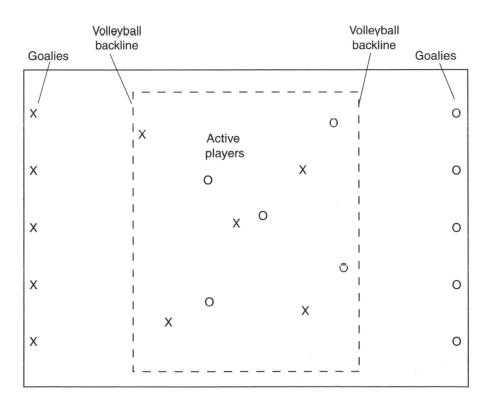

Players score a goal if a kicked ball goes past the basketball end line. Players rotate positions after three minutes.

Hints and Modifications

If players demonstrate good skills in offense and defense, a second ball may be added.

ONE-ON-ONE SOCCER

Overview

In this activity, players practice controlled dribbling and defense in a confined area.

Equipment

- One soccer ball for each group of six students
- Four cone markers of each group of six students

Preparation

- Using cone markers, design one playing area, approximately 15 yards (13.5 meters) long and 15 feet (4.5 meters) wide.
- Assign one group of six players to each area.

Directions

Begin by asking players to pick partners within their assigned groups; partners become opponents. To begin, one pair goes to the center, placing a ball between them. On the "go" signal, play begins with each student trying to gain control and dribble the ball past his end line. Either when a goal is scored or after 30 or 60 seconds of play, a new group comes onto the playing area.

Hints and Modifications

Use a different method of scoring, with the ball successfully passed to a teammate standing behind the team's end line.

VOLLEYBALL BASICS

Overview

Students begin by practicing keeping an object in the air using their hands. Progressions to more realistic volleyball skills follow.

Equipment

- Balloons
- Foam balls
- Beach balls
- Volleyball trainers (These are oversized volleyballs; they are a very common piece of equipment at the elementary or middle-school levels.)

Preparation

- For all grades, begin by giving each student an object: either balloon, foam ball, or beach ball.
- Have the students find personal spaces and be ready to begin practice.

Directions for Kindergarteners and First Graders

Remind the class that all hits must be under control and they must closely follow directions.

1. Keeping both hands about waist high, hold the object in both hands and balance it on your fingertips. After it is balanced, move the hands up to the top of the head and back down again, keeping the ball balanced.
2. Balancing the ball on the fingertips, gently hit it up; balance again and repeat. (The ball should only go a few inches [about 7 centimeters] in the air.)
3. Try both # 1 and # 2 with your hands—even with your chin.
4. With a partner standing approximately 2 feet (.6 meter) away, balance the ball and lightly hit it to your partner. Partners should catch the ball and balance and hit it back.
5. Try # 1 through # 4 with your hands in a "fingers up" position (back of hands toward the floor). Hands should be held at shoulder height.

Directions for Second Graders

Remind the class that all hits must be under control and they should closely follow directions.

1. Review # 2 through #5 of last section.
2. Balance the ball on the fingers; then pass to a partner 3 feet (.9 meter) away, who will catch and balance it.
3. With the hands in a "fingers up" position, have the ball tossed by a partner and catch it.

4. When a ball is tossed lightly, hit it back.

5. Foot work and body position under the ball are essential in volleyball. Keep knees slightly bent, back straight, and hands in the ready position. Have students practice moving to the ball by sliding right, left, forward, and back on your signal—these are reaction drills. When students have moved, say "up" and then make the motions of hitting a ball.

Hints and Modifications

The type of ball used can mean the difference between success and failure. Always allow or recommend students to use a ball that allows them to experience the highest level of success possible.

VOLLEYBALL BASICS

Overview

A progression of simple volleyball skills continues. Place emphasis on correct hitting position and ball contact. Focus on correct setting and bumping technique.

Equipment

- Beach balls
- Volleyball trainers (oversize and regulation size)

Preparation

- Review a correct hitting position—knees bent, back flat, and hands in the ready position.
- Also review the concepts of controlled hitting and hitting rather than catching.
- Present the concept that the direction of your fingers will determine the direction of the ball (e.g., if fingers are down, the ball will go down, if fingers are pointing to the left, the ball will go left).

Directions

Each student should take a partner and be given a ball. Let them choose the type of ball to use in their group. You can make changes in ball usage while monitoring the class.

1. With a partner approximately 5 feet (1.5 meters) away, one partner tosses a ball directly over the head of the receiving student who hits it directly back.

2. Repeat # 1, trying to keep a rally going. If the ball hits the ground or goes beyond the reach of the receiver, stop the rally, gain control, and start again.

3. Present the "bump" shot for any ball coming below chest level. Review the concept of body position and correct hand position: hands open, the bottom hand cupping the top, arms moving slightly to contact the ball, hitting with the heel of the hands, and hitting it back. Review the concept of "where the hands go, the ball will go." Bending the elbows or lifting the arms up during the hit will cause the ball to go backwards, straight up, or too far forward.

4. Have a partner toss the ball at different heights; the partner moves and returns the ball using a set or bump technique.

5. Repeat # 3 and # 4 with partners standing on opposite sides of a net approximately 4 feet (1.2 meters) off the ground.

Hints and Modifications

Stress control and body position; these are the most important aspects of basic instruction for these grade levels. Students need continuous reinforcement that moving to the ball, hitting with both hands, and "calling" for a ball will lead to their success.

VOLLEYBALL SKILL CHALLENGES

Overview

Each series of challenges presents opportunities for skill practice that are motivating and challenging at an individual level.

Equipment

- Balloons
- Beach balls
- Oversized volleyball trainers
- Task cards for each learning area, noting the specific activities for that area. At the primary level, include illustrations of the activities (see form 4.1 on page 71).
- Task check-off card for each student (see form 4.5)

Preparation

- Arrange the gym into three learning areas, placing necessary equipment at each.
- Duplicate task check-off cards for each student and post enlarged task cards at each area.

Directions

Review the concepts of control and using the pads of the fingers to hit the ball. Demonstrate each of the challenge tasks and remind students that they may use any type of ball to accomplish the task.

Hints and Modifications

With younger students, have all students begin work on level one challenges together. As they begin to experience different rates of success, they can separate and begin working independently.

Level One Tasks

Using the pads of the fingers, students should practice hitting the ball upward with two hands.

1. Standing in a hula hoop, set overhead five times.
2. While standing in a hula hoop, clasp hands together and hit the ball in the air three times.
3. Set the ball in the air, clap hands twice, and set it again.
4. Hit a balloon back and forth with a partner five times.

Level Two Tasks

1. Volley the ball overhead three or more times in a row.
2. Bounce the ball on the ground, get under it, and set it back up.
3. Toss the ball into the air above your head and set as high as you can. Repeat four times.
4. Set the ball overhead, turn around, and catch it.
5. Toss a ball into the air and set it into a wall. Catch and repeat five times.

Level Three Tasks

1. With a partner standing 5 feet (1.5 meters) away, set a balloon back and forth five times—hitting with two hands.
2. With a partner standing 5 feet (1.5 meters) away, set a balloon back and forth. After hitting, turn a full circle before returning it.
3. Using a balloon, set the ball while kneeling, stand, and set it back up; go to your knees again and repeat.
4. Try each of the activities above using a volleyball trainer.

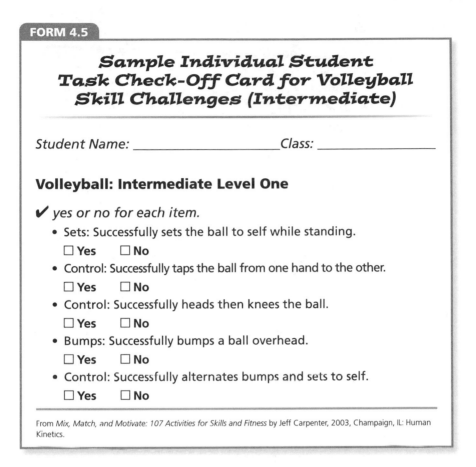

From *Mix, Match, and Motivate: 107 Activities for Skills and Fitness* by Jeff Carpenter, 2003, Champaign, IL: Human Kinetics.

VOLLEYBALL SKILL CHALLENGES

Overview

Each series of challenges presents opportunities for skill practice that are motivating and challenging at an individual level.

Equipment

- Balloons
- Beach balls
- Oversized volleyball trainers
- Task cards for each learning area that note the specific activities for that area. At the primary level, include illustrations of the activities (see form 4.1 on page 71).
- Task check-off card for each student (see form 4.5)

Preparation

- Arrange the gym into three learning areas, placing necessary equipment at each.
- Duplicate a task check-off card for each student and post enlarged task cards at each area.

Level One Tasks

Do the following using a volleyball trainer:

1. Set the ball upward five times in a row while standing in a hula hoop.
2. Toss the ball up with one hand; beginning with the other hand, tap it from one hand to the other while keeping the ball overhead.
3. Holding the hands in position for a "bump," hit the ball in the air three times in a row without catching it.
4. While standing in a hula hoop, bump the ball in the air three times in a row.
5. Alternate sets and bumps, keeping the ball under control.

Level Two Tasks

1. Standing 5 feet (1.5 meters) from a wall, toss the ball into the wall and bump or set it back five times in a row.
2. Beginning on your knees, set the ball, stand, and bump it; kneel again and set.
3. Repeat the last tasks staying within a hula hoop.
4. Standing 5 feet (1.5 meters) from a wall, set the ball into the wall, let it bounce, and bump it back. Alternate sets and bumps.
5. Standing approximately 8 feet (2.4 meters) from a partner, volley a ball back and forth.

Level Three Tasks

1. With a partner, stand 5 feet (1.5 meters) from a wall. Set the ball above the 6-foot (1.8-meter) line; alternate return sets and bumps between partners.
2. Bump the ball up, make a full turn, and repeat five times.
3. Standing with your back toward the wall, toss the ball up and set it backward into the wall. Turn, catch, and repeat.
4. Bump to yourself twice; on the third return, set the ball.
5. Volley the ball against a wall, above the 6-foot (1.8-meter) line, 15 times in a row.

CIRCLE SET

Overview

Circle Set is a fun and challenging activity that allows students to practice skills within a flexible format.

Equipment

- One volleyball trainer for each group of 13 students
- One hula hoop for each student

Preparation

- Arrange game areas for each group of approximately 13 students. Each area consists of an inside and outside circle.
- Place hula hoops in an outer circle, with another set opposite them forming an inner circle.

Directions

Have students stand in each hoop. Players on the inside circle are defense; those on the outside are offense. Students select one player from the offense to stand in the center of the inside hoops. The object is for the offensive players to toss the ball up and set the ball over the heads of the defensive players to their center player. All players except the center must stay in their hoops. If the center player catches the ball, one point is scored for the offense; if the ball hits the ground or is

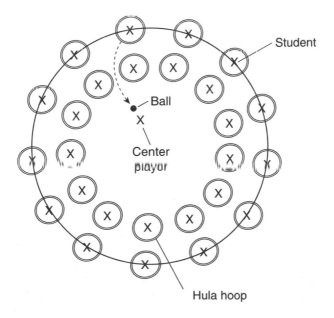

Student

Ball

Center
player

Hula hoop

blocked by the defense, no points are scored. To begin, one offensive team player tosses the ball into the air and attempts a set. After each attempt, another offensive player is given the ball and attempts a toss and set. After all players on the offense have had a turn, the teams switch places.

Hints and Modifications

More advanced players may pass the ball to other players on their team before attempting a pass to the center. For those having difficulty, make the circle smaller; for those having success, make it larger.

FOUR-BALL NEWCOMB

Overview

This is a fast-paced modification of Newcomb. Using four balls, players catch and throw; emphasis is on teamwork and moving under the ball to catch it.

Equipment

- Four volleyball trainers or beach balls for every 12 students
- A net for each playing area
- Four cones for each playing area

Preparation

- Set one low net, 4 to 5 feet (1.2 to 1.5 meters) off the ground for each group of 12 students.
- Mark small playing areas of approximately 25 feet × 15 feet (7.5 meters × 4.5 meters) with cones.
- Divide the class into groups of six, assigning each group to one side of each playing area. Give each team two balls.

Directions

Have players form two lines of three on their side of the area. Explain that each player is responsible for an area approximately one step in each direction from where they are standing. On the "go" signal, players begin throwing and catching the ball. Both balls from each group are thrown at the same time. Remind students that they must be alert to catch balls quickly and throw them back. As soon as a ball is caught, it must be thrown back. If a ball hits the ground or goes out of the marked area, it is considered out of play. The game continues either until all balls are out of play or for four minutes. At the conclusion of each game, players switch from front row to back row and get ready for the next game.

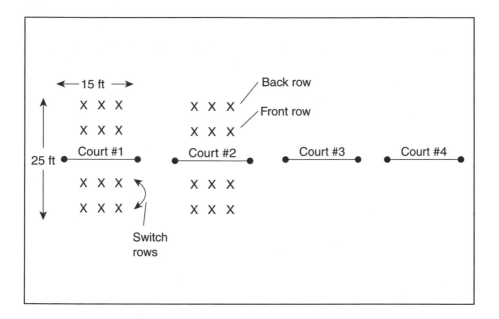

Hints and Modifications

For success, give players the option of setting the ball back rather than catching and throwing. Stress accuracy of throwing — throw to an open space and keep it inbounds.

BUMP AND SET VOLLEYBALL

Overview

Bump and Set Volleyball is a quick game that offers setting and bumping practice without pressuring players to serve.

Equipment

- One court and volleyball trainer for every 12 students

Preparation

- Arrange the necessary courts for each game. Make courts smaller to provide greater opportunity for success and to accommodate additional courts in the gym.
- Vary net heights among grade levels to a maximum of 6 feet (1.8 meters).

Directions

Divide the class into groups of six and assign every two groups to a court. The game begins with one team tossing the ball over the net. The receiving team returns it with either a bump or set. The returning team may hit the ball as many times as necessary to keep the ball in play. If the ball hits the ground, players pick it up and toss it over the net to begin another rally.

Hints and Modifications

As students gain skill, restrict the number of hits made by each team before the ball crosses the net.

VOLLEYBALL ROTATION

Overview

Volleyball Rotation is a motivational game developing bumping and setting skills, teamwork, and cooperation.

Equipment

- One volleyball court
- One volleyball trainer

Preparation

- Arrange one volleyball court; vary net height with the age of students, to a maximum of 6 feet (1.8 meters).
- Divide the class into four equal teams and assign each team to one side of the court.

Directions

Half the players from each team enter the court and form equal lines on each side of the net. The players not on the court stand on the sideline. The game begins with one team tossing the ball over the net. The returning team attempts to hit the ball over the net, with no more than five hits on its side. If the ball hits the ground, goes out of bounds, or is caught, play is stopped and both teams rotate off the court, with new teams entering. Play begins again with a toss.

Hints and Modifications

For more skilled students, a standard-size volleyball trainer may add challenge and enhanced skill practice.

SOFTBALL BASICS

Overview

Softball Basics is a progression of skill-based activities designed to teach and enhance throwing and catching skills.

Equipment

- Yarn balls, "Fleece" balls, "Super Soft" softballs
- Cone markers

Preparation

- Reinforce the concepts of control and accuracy of throwing. Younger students need to understand that control of a throw allows their partner to catch the ball. A hard or long throw is not always the best.

Directions

Students practice throwing as follows:

1. Grip the ball on top with four fingers, the thumb in place under the ball.
2. Practice the concept of opposition—stepping with the opposite foot from the throwing hand. Hold out a hand and step forward with the opposite foot; move to the sequence—elbow back, hand up, step with opposite foot, throw, follow through.
3. Practice throwing the ball into a wall; repeat the directions—elbow back, hand up, step with opposite foot, throw, and follow through.

Students practice catching as follows:

1. Begin in a strong "ready" position: knees slightly bent, feet shoulder width apart, and weight on the balls of the feet.
2. To catch a ball above the waist, hold hands with thumbs together and fingers pointed up.
3. For balls below waist level, hold hands with little fingers together and fingers down.

Students practice batting as follows:

1. Stand with feet parallel to home plate, knees slightly bent.
2. Grip the bat with hands together.

3. Hold the bat at the back of the head and about shoulder height.
4. To swing, rotate shoulders and hips forward as the bat comes around.
5. Keep eyes focused on the ball.

Hints and Modifications

If a student has difficulty catching or appears afraid of the ball, try using a larger ball. Try a playground ball, first rolling it, then tossing it. Progress to a yarn ball, first rolling it, and then tossing it. Keep progressing by changing equipment until the student has success.

SOFTBALL BASICS

Overview

Review and refine basic skills, then add basic game concepts.

Equipment

- Super Soft softballs
- Bats
- Cone markers

Preparation

Set pairs of cone markers approximately 10 feet (3 meters) apart, with a ball for each pair of cones.

Directions

1. Review the basics of throwing and catching (grip, stance, opposition, and "ready" position).
2. Review the basics of batting—grip, stance, swing, and follow-though.
3. Fielding grounders—assume a good ready position, keep your body low with your hands close to the ground, move forward to catch the ball, stand, and throw.
4. Fielding fly balls—assume a good ready position, move in line with the ball, catch the ball above eye level, and throw.
5. Batting—pivot the hips as the bat comes around, keeping your hands in front of the body; snap the wrists and roll hands on the follow-though.

Hints and Modifications

Group students according to ability, changing the practice activity to allow all to be successful. If a student has difficulty in catching, allow him to use a different ball (softer and larger; see the "Hints and Modifications" section on page 102 for more information on this idea).

SOFTBALL SKILL CHALLENGES

Overview

These are motivating and challenging tasks designed to enhance practice in throwing, catching, and batting.

Equipment

- Yarn balls, foam balls, softballs
- Cone markers or bases
- Plastic bats
- Batting tees
- Hula hoops
- Foxtails
- Pole
- Task cards listing the specific activities to be accomplished at the learning area (see form 4.1 on page 71).
- Task check-off card for each student (see form 4.6)

Preparation

- Arrange two practice stations for throwing and catching and one station for batting.

Directions

Explain and demonstrate each task, assign students to a station, and give the "go" signal. As students complete each task, they ask to have it checked so they may move to the next challenge.

Level One Tasks

1. Toss the ball of your choice in the air, clap hands twice, and catch. Repeat 5 times without missing.
2. Throw a ball overhand into a hula hoop taped to a wall 10 feet (3 meters) away. Repeat 10 times.
3. With a partner 10 feet (3 meters) away, roll a ball back and forth 20 times.

FORM 4.6

Sample Individual Student Task Check-Off Card for Softball Skill Challenges (Primary)

Student Name: _____ Class: _____

Softball: Primary Level One Tasks

✔ yes or no for each item.
- Throwing and Catching: Successfully tosses the ball overhead and catches.
  ☐ Yes   ☐ No
- Throwing: Successfully throws overhand into a target.
  ☐ Yes   ☐ No
- Throwing: Successfully throws back and forth to a partner.
  ☐ Yes   ☐ No
- Running: Successfully runs around the bases.
  ☐ Yes   ☐ No

4. Run around the "bases" 4 times, saying the name of each base as touched.

Level Two Tasks

1. Catch a foxtail thrown by a partner 3 times by each color segment. The color segments vary by manufacturer.
2. Catch a fly ball thrown by a partner and throw it back 5 times without a miss.
3. Run around the bases 5 times, touching each with your right foot.
4. Hit a ball off a batting tee into a wall 7 times without a miss.
5. Toss a tennis ball into a wall and catch it 10 times without a miss.

Level Three Tasks

1. Toss a ball 4 to 5 feet (1.2 to 1.5 meters) in the air, turn around, clap your hands, and catch 5 times in a row.
2. Hit a ball suspended from a pole 15 times in a row.

3. Throw a ball into a hula hoop taped to a wall 15 feet (4.5 meters) away 10 times.

4. Throw a ball to a partner 15 feet (4.5 meters) away so that she can catch it without moving to the side, front, or back.

SOFTBALL SKILL CHALLENGES

Overview

Softball Challenges present motivating and challenging tasks designed to enhance throwing, catching, and batting skills.

Equipment

- Yarn balls, foam balls, softballs
- Cone markers or bases
- Plastic bats
- Batting tees
- Hula hoops
- Foxtails
- Pole
- Task cards listing the specific activities to be accomplished at the learning area (See form 4.1 on page 71.)
- Task check-off cards for each student (See form 4.6 on page 104.)

Preparation

- Arrange two learning areas for throwing and catching and one area for batting.

Level One Tasks

1. Catch an overhand throw from a partner 20 feet (6 meters) away 7 times.

2. Toss a ball in the air, sit down, and catch it 10 times.

3. Toss a ball in the air, catch it, and immediately throw overhand to a partner 20 feet (6 meters) away 10 times.

4. Hit a ball off a batting tee and into a wall 10 times without missing.

Level Two Tasks

1. Pitch underhand into a hula hoop taped to a wall 20 feet (6 meters) away 10 times.

2. Toss a ball into the air with your right hand and catch it with your left. Alternate hands 10 times each.

3. Catch a tossed grounder and immediately throw it back to a partner 10 times without a bad throw.

4. Hit five good pitches.

Level Three Tasks

1. Bunt a tossed ball back to a partner standing 10 feet (3 meters) away. Repeat 10 times.

2. Toss a ball in the air, touch the floor with your hands, turn around, and catch it. Repeat 5 times.

3. With a player standing on each base, students begin running the bases. As the runner begins, the catcher throws the ball to first. The ball is thrown around the bases as the runner runs. Each player runs around the bases twice before rotating to a base. Each runner attempts to beat the ball back to home plate.

SOFTBALL TARGETS

Overview

Softball Targets is a fun and challenging activity enhancing throwing skills while reinforcing softball concepts.

Equipment

- Cone markers
- One softball target for each group
- One tennis ball, Wiffle ball, or beanbag for each group
- Score sheet for each group and three markers (poker chips work well; see form 4.7)
- Target: Using a large piece of poster board, draw a 10-inch center circle, then three more concentric circles every six inches. The center circle is a home run, the next a triple, the next a double, and the last a single. Outside the last circle is either a strike or an out.

Preparation

- Tape one target to the wall, with the center of the target approximately waist high for the students.
- Place one cone marker, the score sheet, and the three markers at the throwing line for each group. Vary the throwing line according to the abilities of each class (e.g., a kindergartener's throwing line should be at 5 feet (1.5 meters), a first grader's at 10 to 15 feet (3 to 4.5 meters), and a second grader's at 15 to 20 feet (4.5 to 6 meters).
- Assign four students to each group.

FORM 4.7

Score Sheet for Softball Targets

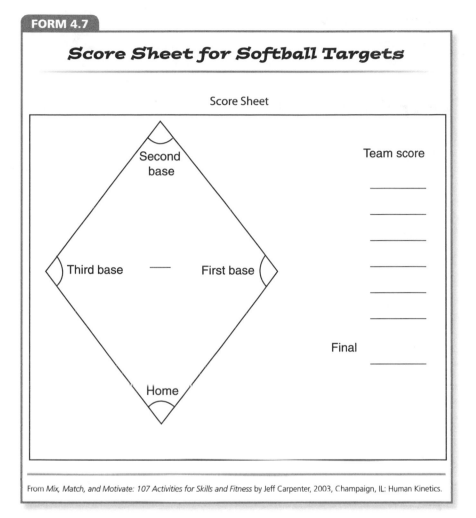

Score Sheet

Second base

Third base   —   First base

Home

Team score

_____

_____

_____

_____

_____

_____

Final

_____

From *Mix, Match, and Motivate: 107 Activities for Skills and Fitness* by Jeff Carpenter, 2003, Champaign, IL: Human Kinetics.

Directions

With each group lined up behind its throwing cone, the first player tosses the ball at the target. The group determines what area of the target was hit and moves its markers on the score sheet. For example, if a single is "thrown," a marker is placed on first base. If the next player throws a double, the first chip is moved to third and the new one is placed on second. The next player throws a single, and the others move forward one base, scoring a run. If the ball misses the target, a strike is recorded. As soon as three outs are made, the team stops, records the number of runs scored, and waits for the group's rotation. The groups rotate either after all have three outs or five minutes have elapsed.

Hints and Modifications

To make the game go faster, "Strike" on the target can be replace with "Out."

BEAT THE BALL

Overview

Whereas most lead-up games at this level consist of kickball and modified T-ball, this activity provides an alternative way to reinforce ball-handling skills and softball concepts.

Equipment

- Cone markers or bases for each base
- Four softballs

Preparation

- Arrange the bases in a diamond, approximately 30 feet (9 meters) apart.
- Divide the class into four equal groups and assign each to a base, including home. Give each group (except for the one at home base) a ball.

Directions

Have players at each base form a line behind the base. The first person in each line holds the ball. On the "go" signal, the first person in line at

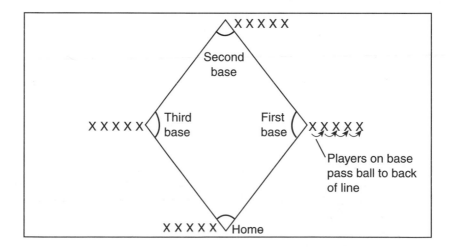

home begins running toward first base. At the same time, the first-base group begins to pass the ball from person to person toward the back of their line. If the runner reaches the base before the ball reaches the last person, a point is scored for the runner's team. As the runner rounds first base, the second-base group begins to pass the ball. This progression continues until the runner reaches home. The running team scores a point if the runner beats the passing team at each base. After all members of the running team have had a turn, the groups rotate bases in a counterclockwise direction.

Hints and Modifications

For kindergarteners, each group may use a playground ball. As players gain skill, spread the base groups out and have them toss the ball to the next person in line.

SOFTBALL POINTS

Overview

Softball Points is a fun activity in which all students can be successful in scoring points for their team while practicing all softball skills in a game situation.

Equipment

- Cones or bases
- Softball
- Bat
- Batting tee

Preparation

- Arrange the playing area with bases placed approximately 30 feet (9 meters) apart.
- Divide the class into two teams.

Directions

The game uses regular softball rules with the following modifications:

1. Batters get as many swings as they need to hit the ball. For an option, use a batting tee as a rule, but pitch to those who request it.
2. When batters hit the ball, they run the bases until thrown out.

3. Each time a runner is safe at a base, a point is scored for that team.

4. After five outs, the teams switch places.

5. After a team reaches 12 points, a new game begins.

Hints and Modifications

Place a cone next to each base. When a runner is safe at a base, the cone in knocked over, which makes it easier to count points.

THREE-TEAM SOFTBALL

Overview

Three-Team Softball is an excellent game for practicing softball skills in a fun and fast-moving format.

Equipment

- Cones or bases
- Softball
- Bat
- Optional: batting tee

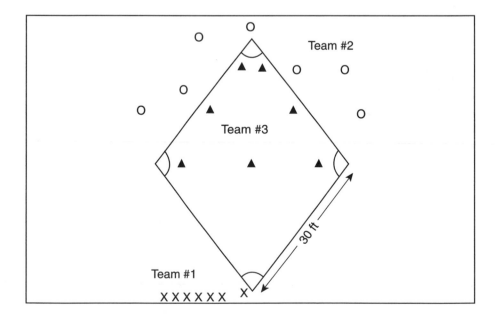

Preparation

- Arrange the playing area as you would a regular softball field, with bases about 30 feet (9 meters) apart.
- Divide the class into three equal groups.

Directions

Assign each of the three groups to a different location on the field: group 1 to the outfield, group 2 to the infield, and group 3 to batting. Batting may be done off a tee or with the teacher pitching. Apply regular softball rules, with the following exceptions:

1. After all players on the batting team have batted, teams rotate from batting to outfield, outfield to infield, infield to batting.
2. Points are scored for each base reached by a runner. This allows all players to be part of the team scoring process.

Hints and Modifications

Reduce the number of players on each team by having two playing areas. This will allow for enhanced activity and greater participation (e.g. 5 players on each team instead of 10).

FLOOR HOCKEY BASICS

Overview

Because it is directly aligned with soccer, floor hockey provides a natural progression of concepts and skills, moving from the development of foot–eye to hand–eye coordination skills.

Equipment

- Floor hockey sticks
- Beanbags
- Milk cartons
- Yarn balls

Preparation

- Give each student a stick and a beanbag, milk carton, or yarn ball.
- Remind students that any time, including when they are standing still, the blade of the stick comes above knee level, it is "high sticking." High sticking called the first time results in a warning; the

second time, the student must sit out for a period of time. If a third high sticking is called on a student, he should be excluded for the remainder of the day.

• When gripping the stick, place the top hand within a few inches of the top, with the lower hand at mid stick or a bit lower. The thumbs on both hands should be on the front of the stick, pointing toward the ground.

Directions for Kindergarteners and First Graders

1. Standing with the beanbag or milk carton directly in front of them, students tap one side of the object, then the other; they then place the stick on top of the object. They should say, "right, left, top," and repeat.

2. Students tap the object from side to side. On the stop signal, they place the stick on top of the object.

3. Students tap the object from side to side, while moving forward. On the stop signal, they place the stick on top of the object.

4. Moving around the area, give the direction to reverse. When you have given the signal, the students step to the other side of the object, turn, and begin moving again.

5. With a partner standing approximately 6 feet (1.8 meters) away, students pass the object back and forth.

6. After students have successfully performed the skills noted here using a beanbag or milk carton, they should repeat using a yarn ball.

Directions for Second Graders

1. Repeat all of the previous directions, using a softball-sized Wiffle ball. Stress the importance of maintaining control of the ball. Any time the "stop" signal is given, students should be able to reach out with their stick and stop the ball.

2. Set cones against a wall, approximately 4 feet (1.2 meters) apart. From 15 feet (4.5 meters) away, students move the ball toward the cones, stop approximately 6 feet (1.8 meters) away, and shoot at the goal.

3. Students pass the ball back and forth with a partner while moving around the area. They should keep approximately 6 feet (1.8 meters) apart. Stress practicing passing in front of the person, which enables them to continue moving forward; add taking a shot, using the cone goals against a wall.

Hints and Modifications

- As students move from one level to the next, you may need to modify the equipment. Students beginning the third level may need to begin with milk cartons before using a ball or puck.
- Always stress control; if the ball or puck is out of reach, it is out of the students' immediate control.

FLOOR HOCKEY BASICS

Overview

Progressions continue, focusing on ball control and teamwork.

Equipment

- Floor hockey stick for each student
- Wiffle ball for each student. The players use Wiffle balls instead of plastic floor hockey pucks to create a faster game and necessitate greater stick movement and control.

Preparation

- Review skills successfully performed at the primary level.
- Reinforce the concept and rules of high-sticking and the need to focus on control.
- The blade of the stick should be pointed in the direction the player is moving as the student taps the ball from side to side. Emphasize that they should not sweep or push the ball.

Directions

Each student should have a stick and Wiffle ball. Review the second grade-level skills for using a Wiffle ball (see "Directions for Second Graders" on page 112).With a partner, students should do the following:

1. One partner moves the ball around the other partner. Partners should be doing jumping jacks while the ball is being moved around them.
2. Partners stand with feet apart while their partners pass the ball between their feet, run around them, and stop the ball within one step of them. Partners reverse roles and repeat.
3. Arrange 12 to 15 cones randomly around the gym. Each student has a stick and ball. When you give the "go" signal, players begin dribbling around the area, avoiding cones and other players.

When you give the "stop" signal, players reach out and stop their ball within one step. If the ball can't be stopped within the step, it cannot be stopped. On the "go" signal, students return to their ball and begin dribbling.

4. With their partners standing 6 feet (1.8 meters) from a goal marked by cones against a wall, students move forward and complete a pass. The receiving partner immediately shoots at the goal.

Hints and Modifications

Stress control of the ball or puck at all times. Define specific areas, using poly spots or cones, that students must stay within.

FLOOR HOCKEY SKILL CHALLENGES

Overview

These are motivational challenges designed to enhance levels of skill and understanding.

Equipment

- Floor hockey stick (For primary students, a 36-inch or 42-inch [93-centimeter or 106.7-centimeter] stick cut in half works well.)
- Milk carton or yarn ball for each student
- Cone markers
- Task cards listing specific activities at the learning area (see form 4.1 on page 71). Use illustrations to show the activities for the primary grades.
- Task check-off card for each student (see form 4.8)

Preparation

- Develop task cards for each area.
- Arrange two learning areas.

Directions

Review concepts and expectations while describing and demonstrating tasks at each station. Assign students to stations and give the "go" signal.

Level One Tasks

1. Keep control of a yarn ball while moving to a cone 15 feet (4.5 meters) away. Circle the cone and return.

FORM 4.8

Sample Individual Student Task Check-Off Card for Floor Hockey Skill Challenges (Intermediate)

Student Name: _____ Class: _____

Floor Hockey Intermediate Level One

✔ *yes or no for each item.*

- Passing and Dribbling: Successfully receives a pass and begins a controlled dribble.
  ☐ **Yes**   ☐ **No**
- Dribbling: Successfully dribbles through a series of cones.
  ☐ **Yes**   ☐ **No**
- Shooting: Successfully dribbles toward a goal and shoots.
  ☐ **Yes**   ☐ **No**
- Goal Keeping: Successfully blocks a shot on the goal.
  ☐ **Yes**   ☐ **No**

From *Mix, Match, and Motivate: 107 Activities for Skills and Fitness* by Jeff Carpenter, 2003, Champaign, IL: Human Kinetics.

2. Pass the ball to a partner standing 10 feet (3 meters) away. The partner should not move her feet to receive the ball.
3. Pass to a partner using alternating forehand and backhand passes.
4. Standing 10 feet (3 meters) from a goal, make five shots.

Level Two Tasks

1. While standing still, feet apart, move the ball between your feet, back to the front.
2. Pass to a partner, who is moving.
3. Dribble the ball and pass to a stationary partner.
4. Beginning 15 feet (4.5 meters) from a goal, move toward the goal and shoot when 6 feet (1.8 meters) away.

Level Three Tasks

1. Maintain control while weaving through a series of cones.
2. Dribble through a series of cones, turn at the first cone, and pass to a partner standing nearby.

3. Move with a partner down the floor, passing a ball back and forth. Keep 6 feet (1.8 meters) apart.

4. As a goalie, block shots taken from 6 feet (1.8 meters) away.

FLOOR HOCKEY SKILL CHALLENGES

Overview

These are motivational challenges designed to enhance levels of skill and understanding.

Equipment

- Floor hockey stick (For primary students, a 36-inch or 42-inch [93-centimeter or 106.7-centimeter] stick cut in half works well.)
- Milk carton or yarn ball for each student
- Cone markers
- Task cards listing specific activities at the learning area (see form 4.1 on page 71). Use illustrations to show the activities for the primary grades.
- Task check-off card for each student (see form 4.8 on page 115)

Preparation

- Create task cards for each area.
- Arrange two learning areas.

Level One Tasks

Review level-two and level-three tasks from the primary level using a Wiffle ball (see "Floor Hockey Skill Challenges" on page 114).

1. Receive a pass from a partner, dribble around him, return to the starting point, and pass.

2. Dribble the ball through a series of cones placed 3 feet (1.2 meters) apart.

3. From 15 feet (4.5 meters) away, dribble toward a goal and shoot from 10 feet (3 meters) away.

4. As a goalie, block shots taken from 10 feet (3 meters) away.

Levels Two and Three Tasks

Levels are combined in a series of partner activities:

1. With a partner, steal the ball while both of you are moving.

2. Standing in a 10-foot (3-meter) circle, play one-on-one with a partner. A point is scored when the ball is moved, under control, out of the circle, and stopped within one step.
3. Move with a partner down the floor, passing the ball immediately after receiving it.
4. Passing back and forth with a partner, move toward a goal, and take a shot from 10 feet (3 meters) away.
5. Take shots from different angles while moving in front of a goal, passing, and receiving.

Hints and Modifications

As students progress, change the type of objects they use. Continue to reinforce the rules of high-sticking and the need to keep control of the ball at all times.

HOCKEY BANDITS

Overview

Hockey Bandits is a fun and fast-moving game for total class participation. It reinforces skills of offense and defense.

Equipment

- A floor hockey stick for each student
- Softball-size Wiffle ball for each student

Preparation

- Remind students of rules for high-sticking and the need to be in control at all times.

Directions

Give each student a floor hockey stick; all but four players are also given a ball. On the "go" signal, all players begin moving around the area. The players who do not have a ball are "bandits." The objective is for the bandits to steal a ball and gain control. If a bandit steals another player's ball, that player becomes a bandit and attempts to steal a ball.

Hints and Modifications

To keep this exciting game moving, give the "stop" signal every 30 seconds. At that time assign "new" players to the role of bandit.

TEAM RACE HOCKEY

Overview

While focusing on control and speed, skills of dribbling and agility are enhanced.

Equipment

- One floor hockey stick for each group of six students
- One cone marker for each student

Preparation

- Using the cone markers, make a circle for each group of six students.
- Place a floor hockey stick and ball at each circle.

Directions

Assign one student from each group of six to stand by that group's cone. Each player in the group takes a number between 1 and 6. Player # 1 picks up the stick and ball and returns to his cone. On the "go" signal, player # 1 begins to dribble around the circle; when returning to his cone, he passes the stick and ball to player # 2. Each player in turn dribbles around the circle. When all players have made a complete circle, the group sits down.

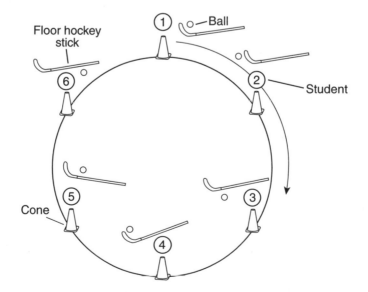

Hints and Modifications

- Have students weave in and out of other players as they move around the circle.
- Do not have students take a number in consecutive order. With random numbering, the player finishing the circle must move to another spot to pass the stick. Have her call the name of the player she is passing to.

NEW BALL HOCKEY

Overview

This game involves all hockey skills in a fast team-oriented game.

Equipment

- Six hockey sticks
- Two different colored balls

Preparation

- Review the rules of high-sticking and the concepts of passing and teamwork.

Directions

Divide the class into two groups, each standing on opposite sides of the playing area. To begin, three players from each team come to the center line. One team is assigned red sticks, the other yellow. The object is to gain and maintain control of the ball, pass it among team members, and move it across the assigned goal line.

On the "go" signal, play begins, with one team taking possession and attempting to move the ball. The other team tries to steal and gain control, thereby moving the ball to its goal line. During the play, call "new ball" and drop the second ball into play. At that time, players must leave the ball they are playing and begin playing the new ball. Call "new ball" about every 15 to 30 seconds. After a goal is scored or 2 minutes have elapsed, new players rotate into the game.

Hints and Modifications

Call "new ball" when players are close to scoring; drop the ball at the center line or at the opposite end of the area.

FLOOR HOCKEY SOFTBALL

Overview

This is an interesting game, which, as its name implies, combines the concepts of softball with the skills of hockey. Teamwork is emphasized together with skills of passing and dribbling.

Equipment

- Four cone markers
- Floor hockey sticks for half the class, plus one
- Two Wiffle balls

Preparation

- Arrange the cones as for a softball game.

Directions

Divide the class into half, with one group fielding and the other "batting." The members of the fielding group take hockey sticks to their positions. One ball is placed at home base and the other is placed at first base.

To begin, the first player up hits the ball toward the field (with no high-sticking) and runs the bases carrying the stick. When reaching

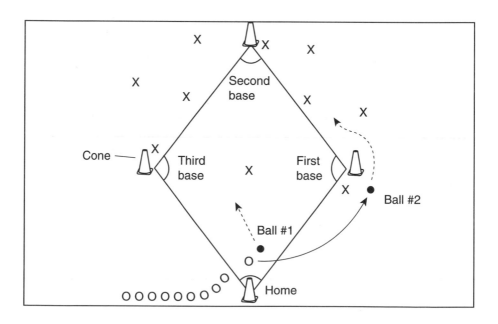

first base, he begins to dribble the ball found there around the other bases. The fielding team must get the ball that was "batted" and pass it to the first-base player, who begins passing it around to the other bases until it gets home.

The runner gets one point for each base rounded before the ball reaches home. Play continues until everyone on the batting team has had a turn.

Hints and Modifications

The fielding team may pass the ball directly home to stop the runner rather than pass the ball around all the bases. Award points to the runner's team for each base passed before the ball reaches home.

BALANCING UNIT

Overview

Balancing activities are both fun and challenging for students. Use various equipment and present activities in a motivational progression.

Sample Equipment

- Stilts
- Pogo balls
- Pogo sticks
- Balance boards
- Balance disks
- Unicycles

Preparation

- Arrange equipment in a learning area format, providing appropriate room for each activity.
- While students will work independently, close supervision is required to ensure directions and all safety precautions are being followed.

Directions

Activities presented in this section are used as examples and also to spark each teacher's imagination and creativity. Determine specific tasks and equipment to be used based on the availability of equipment and the needs of the students.

Stilts

Use small foam stilts for younger students, progressing to larger stilts for more experienced students.

Against a wall, place stilts approximately shoulder width apart; place hands on the stilts with arms extended down the shaft. Place one foot on the stilt, then the other, with your back straight and weight evenly distributed. Take support away from the wall and balance—repeat several times.

After balancing in a stationary position, students may begin moving forward. To move, lift with the arm and hand, taking the weight off the foot, as when taking a step, while maintaining contact with the foot-rest. The focus should be on taking small steps, keeping back straight, and keeping feet or stilts shoulder width apart.

When stepping or falling off, students should remain in control, stepping off as they begin to loose their balance. If they lean forward and continue jumping they may fall out of control and/or put pressure on the lower part of the stilt, possibly breaking the stilt. The following is a progression of activities that will aid in skill development:

1. Balance against the wall.
2. Move forward.
3. Move forward, stop, and start again.
4. Move forward, weaving through a series of cones.
5. Move forward, turn a circle, and move forward again.
6. Move forward, stop, and move backward.

Pogo Sticks

Use sturdy pogo sticks appropriate for the size and weight of the students. A pogo stick designed for heavier students will only lead to frustration for lighter students.

Use pogo balls before using a pogo stick. The same progressions apply. However, when mounting the ball, place one foot on the down side, instep against the ball, and place the other foot on the top, instep against the ball. Slowly move to a balancing position while pinching the ball between the feet.

The initial progression is very similar to that used for stilts. Standing against a wall, hold the handles of the pogo close to the hips; place one foot on, then the other. Balance for several seconds and hop off with both feet. Students must learn to hop off under control with both feet to ensure their safety and avoid putting pressure on the pogo support, which might cause it to break.

Keeping the pogo close to the body, begin by pushing down with both feet, allowing the spring to cause the rebound effect, facilitating hopping.

Mounting the pogo away from the wall is basically the same as mounting it against the wall, except students jump on the feet supports (both feet at the same time) and immediately experience the rebound and begin hopping. Progressions include the following:

1. Balance against a wall.
2. Hop forward.
3. Hop forward while weaving through a cone maze.
4. Hop to the side, in circles, in various combinations and patterns.
5. Add a jump rope for highly skilled students. First practice with a pogo ball, follow by hopping on the pogo stick without using the hands.

Balance Boards and Balance Disks

These include commercially made and homemade flat boards, roller boards, and disks. These are excellent for helping primary students experience both static and dynamic balance. Have students stand and balance on each piece of equipment. After they can balance consistently, add the following challenges:

1. Toss a beanbag from one hand to the other.
2. Toss a beanbag in the air and catch it.
3. Toss a beanbag to a partner.
4. Bounce a ball with one hand, moving the ball from side to side.
5. Using a balance disk, turn in circles and either toss beanbags or bounce balls while turning.

Unicycles

Unicycles are a great deal of fun and a source of motivation and challenge for all students. Using the proper size cycle is important. As when riding bicycles, a leg should be extended, knee slightly bent, when the pedal is in the down position.

Against a wall, place the right pedal at the "nine o'clock" position and straddle the seat, with the wheel slightly in front. Place the right foot on the pedal; push down. This causes the wheel to go back into the wall. Place the left foot lightly on the pedal (put no weight on the pedal). Weight must be on the seat, not on the pedals. Maintain balance against the wall.

When dismounting, lean forward, stepping off with the "up" foot—in this case the left foot. Reach behind and hold the seat; step off under control. Stepping off under control is extremely important and should be practiced and reinforced throughout the progression.

The use of spotters is an important component when moving away from the wall. Spotters should be on each side of the rider. They do not touch the rider; instead, they act as supports. With spotters standing to the side and slightly in front of the rider, the rider extends her arms to lightly touch the shoulder of each spotter. As the rider begins to pedal forward, the spotters move with her—the rider determines the pace.

To begin moving forward, the rider, using the support of spotters, begins a steady and controlled pedal forward. Reinforce the important concept that the weight remains on the seat, not on the pedals. After students successfully balance against the wall and dismount, the following progression may be followed:

1. Move forward one pedal, stop, balance, and move forward again.
2. Slowly, using a steady rate of pedaling, move forward.
3. Mount the unicycle away from the wall. Using spotters, put the right pedal in the down position, place the right foot on the pedal and weight on the seat, and step up with the left foot.
4. When moving forward, lift the hands on the spotters' shoulders—spotters must keep moving with the rider.
5. Using the spotters as a pivot, make a turn.
6. As the students progress to this point, only additional practice is required to allow them to ride without spotters.

Hints and Modifications

Balancing units are fun and exciting for all students. Allow students to progress at their own pace while using your imagination to create additional tasks and challenges once students have successfully performed the basics. When using a station format, have the students rotate every five minutes to avoid frustration. Unicycles should either be used as a station or as a separate lesson. It is suggested that the balance unit be done for two days and unicycles presented separately for another three days. Students progress quickly on the unicycles and want to continue.

It's Time to Close

Motivators to Bring Them Back

At the end of each lesson, you should present to students activities that take little organization, are fun, and are familiar. Make this a time when expectations for skill and fitness development can be lowered and students can just have fun moving and being active.

Fun and Challenging: That's How to End

During this time, present low-organization games, cooperative games, and fun individual challenges. After participating in these activities, students should have a feeling of accomplishment from their efforts. It is extremely important that students work hard toward accomplishing tasks and challenges presented during the other components of each lesson. During the closing activity component, however, all students should experience success and rekindle the natural desire to return another day.

Closing Activities

The activities presented in this chapter involve little instruction and organization. You may include relays, individual and small group challenges, noncompetitive games, and cooperative activities in the 5- to 7-minute closing period.

GROUPS OF ANIMALS

Overview

Students move together in groups, using various animal walks and making animal sounds.

Equipment

- One poly spot marker for each group

Preparation

- Have students separate into groups of three, either in a line formation or together in a semicircle formation around a "home base" (the poly spot marker).
- Explain that they must move together doing the animal walks and that they can make the sound of the animal and play (safely) like the animals might play.

Directions

After arranging the students in groups, call out the name of the first animal (e.g., seal). While staying in their groups, all students begin doing a seal walk and making sounds like seals. For this one, you could put a beach ball by each group and have group members toss and balance it like a seal might. After about 30 seconds, the group moves back to its home base and waits for another animal name to be called.

Hints and Modifications

- Other animals to use include bear, crab, elephant, kangaroo, dog, lion, and rabbit.
- Have the students select animals: Give each group a chance to call out an animal name.

ALLIGATOR HUNTER TAG

Reprinted, by permission, from J.D. Poppen, Alligator's tail tag. In *The Best of Games That Come Alive* (Puyallup, WA: Action Productions).

Overview

This is a cooperative tag game involving cooperation and challenges for the group.

Equipment

- One football flag for each group

Preparation

- Arrange students in groups of 10 or 11.
- Have each group form a line, with each member's arms around the waist of the person in front of him. The last person in line tucks a football flag in the back of her belt.

Directions

On the "go" signal, the head of the alligator—the first person in line—starts to chase the tail—the last person in line. All students in the line must work together to prevent the head from catching the tail. If the alligator catches the tail—by pulling the flag—the head becomes the tail, and the second person in line becomes the new head. If the line breaks, the group must stop, jump up and down ten times, reconnect, and begin again.

Hints and Modifications

Older students or those groups who have caught their own tails can try to catch another alligator's tail. If the group succeeds, its head becomes the tail of the new alligator. If all of one group's members attach to other alligators, that group can be declared the "top gator" for the day.

WHAT'RE YOU DOING?

Overview

This movement twist on the game of charades provides leadership and action.

Equipment

- None

Preparation

- Divide the class into groups of seven or eight, and have each form a circle.
- Explain that physical activity can take many forms, such as playing games, walking with family and friends, and raking leaves.

Directions

Ask one student in each group to move into the center of his circle and become the first group leader. On the "go" signal, the leader begins to demonstrate a physical movement or activity. The others in the group imitate the activity. After approximately 20 seconds, call out, "Guess." Students in each circle then guess what activity is demonstrated. The first student to name the activity moves to the center and becomes the new leader. Students repeat the rotation until each student has had at least one turn as group leader.

Hints and Modifications

It may be difficult for the leader to determine who was first to identify the movement to become the new leader. If this is the case, establish a rotation system so that everyone has a turn as leader.

JUMP THE RIVERS

Overview

This is a fun and challenging activity involving basic locomotor movements in various combinations.

Equipment

- 26 to 30 jump ropes

Preparation

- Place parallel sets of jump ropes approximately 2 feet (.6 meter) apart around the gym.
- Have students find an open space and get ready to "jump the rivers."

Directions

Before the students begin to move, tell them that each set of parallel jump ropes is a river that they must jump as they move around the gym. If they land in a river, they must do 10 jumping jacks and then begin moving again.

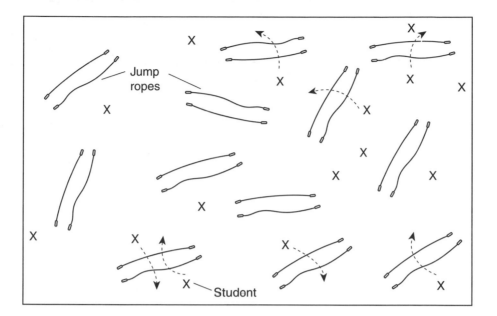

On the "go" signal, students begin a teacher-selected locomotor movement (such as skipping, running, or galloping) to jump every "river" they come to. Change the locomotor movement every 30 seconds.

Hints and Modifications

- If a student moves a "river," leave it in its new position. The river has changed course.
- Have the students move in pairs or groups of three while holding hands.

THE GREAT RACE

Overview

This fast-paced running activity involves team and individual work.

Equipment

- Poly spots or cone markers

Preparation

- Place a series of poly spots or cone markers—one for every two students—on a sideline of the gym. Markers should be approximately 3 feet (.9 meter) apart.
- Have each student find a partner and stand behind a marker.

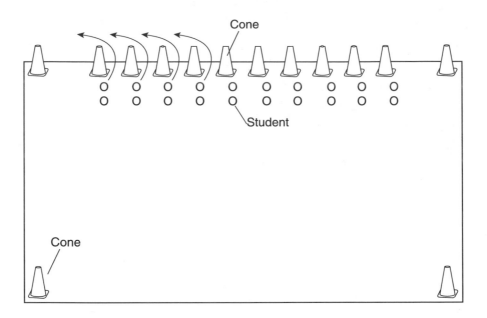

Directions

On the "go" signal, one person in each group leaves his marker and begins to run around the perimeter of the gym. During the run, call out, "Fill it up." When they hear that direction, all running students do 15 jumping jacks and then continue running. When the runner gets back to his marker, he gives his partner a high-five, and each does 5 push-ups or curl-ups. After they complete the exercise, the next partner begins her run.

Hints and Modifications

Have both partners run at the same time while holding onto a plastic baseball bat or jump rope. When they get back to their marker, they perform the push-up or curl-up routine and begin another running sequence.

SPELL AND PASS

Overview

This is a challenging game that combines spelling with catching and throwing skills.

Equipment

- One playground ball or volleyball for each group of students

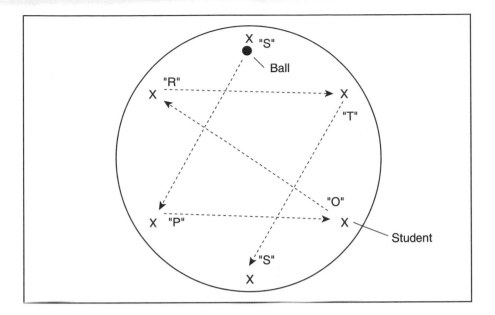

Preparation

- Divide the class into groups of six or seven students.
- Have each group form a circle, and give each circle a ball.

Directions

To begin the activity, call out a word. The student with the ball says the first letter of the word and passes the ball to another student, who says the second letter. The pattern continues until the word is spelled. If the group misspells the word, they must go back to the first letter and make the correction.

Hints and Modifications

- Give a different word to each group.
- Try math problems: The first person repeats the problem, and the others in the group say the answer as the ball is passed to everyone in the circle.

THE GREAT CIRCLE CHASE

Overview

This is a simple relay race that provides competition and challenges.

Equipment

• None (except when using modifications)

Preparation

- Divide the class into equal groups of 10 to 15 students.
- Arrange each group in a large circle.
- Designate one person in each circle to begin the relay.

Directions

On the "go" signal, the designated person in each circle begins to run, skip, or gallop around the outside of her circle. When she completes her turn, she tags the next person, who begins his lap. After all students have completed two turns, the entire team stands, does five jumping jacks, and sits down. The first team to finish wins.

Hints and Modifications

Have students sit or kneel on scooters to complete their laps around the circle.

CHALLENGES FOR TODAY

Overview

Individual and partner tasks involve balance and skill designed to challenge and motivate each student.

Equipment

• None

Preparation

- Have students find a personal space within the boundaries of the facility.
- Remind the students that tasks will be simple for some and more difficult for others. Every person should attempt the task for the day and work at his or her own pace for success.

Directions

Have all students attempt one or two challenges for the day.

- Stork stand: While standing, students fold their arms across their chests, slowly lift one leg, and place the sole of the foot on the side of the knee of the supporting leg. They can also try this with the other leg and with their eyes closed.

- Balance touch: Students take pieces of paper, crumple them into balls, and place the balls on the floor approximately 2 feet (.6 meter) in front of them. While balancing on one foot, students reach forward, touch the paper, and return to a standing position. They can repeat this while balancing on the other foot, or they can move the paper farther out or closer depending on their success.

- Three-point tip-up: Using mats, students squat down with hands flat, fingers pointing forward, and elbows inside and pressed against their knees. They slowly lean forward pressing against their knees and their taking weight on their hands until their heads touch the mat. Balance for five seconds or more.

- Frog stand: This is similar to three-point tip-up, except that the head never touches the mat. (See page 40.)

- Partner hop: Students hop for short distances with partners or using one or more of the following combinations:

   1. Stand facing each other and holding hands. Hop forward or backward 4 steps, hop to one side, and then hop the other 4 steps.
   2. Stand side by side with inside arms around each other's waist. Hop 10 steps forward on the outside foot.
   3. Stand back to back and gently lock elbows. Hop forward or backward 4 steps.

Stork stand.

Balance touch.

- Wring the dish rag: Partners face each other and hold hands. Together, they raise one arm and turn under that arm. They continue turning until they are back in their original position. They should repeat this action in the opposite direction by raising the other arm.

Hints and Modifications

Keep this activity fun and challenging. If students or groups accomplish a task quickly, suggest a more difficult modification—asking the group how to increase difficulty levels works well.

MOVE IT

Overview

Students work together to pass one or two balls around a circle as quickly as possible.

Equipment

- One or two playground balls for each group

Preparation

- Divide students into groups of 10 to 12, and have each group form a large circle.
- Give each group one or two playground balls. Give balls to students on opposite sides of the circle.

Directions

On the "go" signal, the students holding the balls turn to those on their right and pass the balls while they say, "Go." The students on the right then turn to their right, pass the ball, and say, "Go." Each student follows the same pattern, passing the ball as quickly as possible. After 30 seconds, give the signal to change direction.

Hints and Modifications

- Try using different pieces of equipment to pass—one ball and one beanbag, or a beanbag and a plastic bowling pin.
- Try timing each group to determine how long it takes to get around the circle. Have the groups try to beat their previous times.

THE GREAT BALL WALK

Overview

This fun cooperative activity stresses team work, movement skills, and flexibility in trying to move a large cage ball from one place to another.

Equipment

- One cage ball per group

Preparation

- Organize students into groups of six or seven. If possible, give each group a large cage ball.

Directions

Place the cage ball in the center of the circle, and have the group form a circle around the ball, holding it with their bodies. Students cannot use their hands at any time. The group must lift the ball by pushing against it and not allowing it to touch the floor. After the ball is off the ground, the challenge is to move it from the center of the gym to the end line.

Hints and Modifications

Set up cones for the group to weave around or obstacles to step over while moving across the floor.

FULL-COURT LEAP FROG

Overview

Students work together in groups of six to eight in this cooperative and challenging version of Leap Frog.

Equipment

- None

Preparation

- Students should know how to perform a leap-frog activity before participating in this progressive activity.
- Review safety precautions (i.e., solid support position, head tucked, and hands placed on shoulders when going over) with all students.

Directions

Students line up single-file in their groups, facing the same direction. Each student takes a squat position with her shoulders up, elbows straight, and head tucked. The last student in line begins to leap-frog over the other students in succession until she reaches the front of the line. After leaping the last student in line, she assumes the squat position. As soon as she has cleared the third person in line, the next person begins to leap. This rotation continues until the group reaches the end line opposite from their starting point.

Hints and Modifications

For more highly skilled groups, have the entire class form a circle that is open at one end. With larger groups, more students will be leaping, allowing for more fun and activity.

SQUEEZE PLAY

Overview

This is a challenging and cooperative activity for the entire class. Students must move together and communicate to succeed.

Equipment

* None

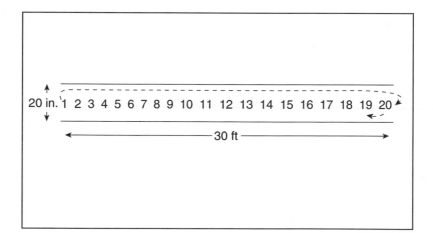

Preparation

- Draw two parallel lines about 20 inches (50.8 centimeters) apart and 30 feet (9 meters) long (long enough to fit the entire class when students stand close to each other).

Directions

Students stand inside the two parallel lines and count off. On the "go" signal, they must reverse their number order without stepping outside the lines.

Hints and Modifications

Try the activity once without the lines for practice. This will allow the students to understand the concept and requirements of reversing their numeric order.

TRIO TAG

Overview

This tag game requires teamwork, concentration, and fast-paced action.

Equipment

- None

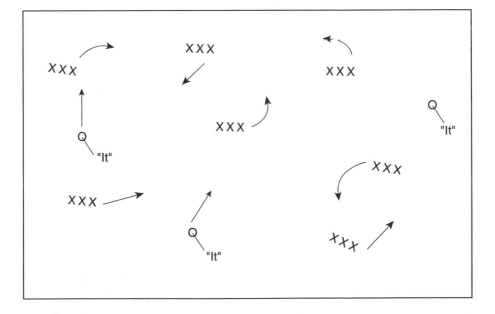

Preparation

- Divide students into groups of three or four. Have each group find a space away from others.
- Choose three students to be "it." These students will attempt to tag others lightly on the shoulder.

Directions

In their groups, students lie on their bellies shoulder to shoulder, facing the same direction. On the "go" signal, one student from each group and the students chosen to be "it" stand up and begin running. The students from the groups attempt to lie down at the end of other groups. If tagged, runners become "it." If runners are successful in lying down at the end of other groups, the student on the opposite end of the group must stand and begin running.

Hints and Modifications

- To keep students from tagging too hard, give the "it" students foam disks or Nerf footballs. They must hold on to the object and tag the runner lightly on the shoulder with it.
- Caution runners not to move over people lying on the ground.
- Try changing running to skipping, galloping, or sliding.

BEANBAG GRAB

Overview

This is an action-packed team activity with some competition and a lot of movement.

Equipment

- As many beanbags or small balls as are available—at least 50
- Timer or stopwatch

Preparation

- Divide the class into two groups and have each sit in line at opposite ends of the gym about 3 feet (.9 meter) beyond the end line.
- Place all the objects along one end line.

Directions

On the "go" signal, start the clock. Students at one end run to the opposite end, pick up one object, and return it to their end line. They repeat this until they have picked up all objects. When all objects are on the end line and students are sitting down, stop the stopwatch and record the time. The other team then tries to beat the first time.

Hints and Modifications

- Caution students to look before they run. After picking up an object, they should turn and look to make sure that nobody is coming toward them before they run.
- Objects must be laid on the end line, not tossed at it.
- Give each team two attempts to better its time or to beat the best time.

ROCK, PAPER, SCISSORS TAG

Overview

This is a fast-paced tag game based on an old favorite.

Equipment

- Poly spot markers (optional)

Preparation

- Have each student find a partner. Partners stand facing each other on the center line of the gym.
- Place markers on the line approximately 2 feet (.6 meter) apart, giving each group a home base. Students should stand one big step away from the spot (optional) or line.
- Explain the "Rock, Paper, Scissors" concept: rock dulls scissors, paper covers rock, and scissors cut paper.

Directions

With students facing each other and their feet facing the center line, count 1, 2, 3. On 3, students show either rock, paper, or scissors. The losing student begins to run toward the end line behind her, and her partner attempts to tag her lightly on the shoulder before she reaches her line. If successful in reaching the line, the runner gets one point. Students then return to the center line for another attempt.

Hints and Modifications

- Caution students not to tag hard and to remain under control at all times.
- Change from running to skipping or galloping.

SIT ON MY KNEE TAG

Overview

This simple tag game involves cooperation and fast-paced movement.

Equipment

- None

Preparation

- Designate three or four students to be "it." Have all students spread out within designated boundaries.

Directions

On the "go" signal, students begin running, remaining under control and within the boundaries. If tagged, a student stops and kneels on the floor with one knee up. If another student comes to him, sits on his knee, and shakes hands while sitting, the tagged student is free to stand up and begin running again.

Hints and Modifications

- To involve more students in the challenges of being "it," rotate students every 30 to 40 seconds.
- Give "it" students foam Frisbees or Nerf footballs to tag with. They must hold the object and tag lightly on the shoulder. This eliminates possible hard tags and pushing.

WHAT'RE YOU DOING—TOO?

Overview

This is a modification of "What're You Doing?" for primary grades. Activities and movements used at the intermediate level should be more detailed and more challenging in movement and in creativity. This is a creative game involving leadership and cooperation within a group.

Equipment

- None

Preparation

- Divide the class into groups of six or seven, and have each group form a large circle.
- Have one student from each group go to the center of the circle.

Directions

On the "go" signal, the student in the center begins to perform the movements of a physical activity, but not necessarily a sport. Shoveling snow, fishing, and biking are great ideas. Students in the outer circle begin performing the movements and try to guess the activity. The first student who guesses the activity goes to the center, where the student leaving the center tells her what activity she must show. Students leaving the center cannot guess the activity that the new student is performing. The rotation continues until time is called.

Hints and Modifications

Encourage students to think and show a variety of activities. This activity is designed to help students think of physical activity involving more than just sports or activities they do in class.

TEAM BALLOON VOLLEY

Overview

This skill development or review activity is designed as a basic challenge or as part of a volleyball lesson.

Equipment

- One balloon or beach ball for each group of six or seven students

Preparation

- Divide students into groups of six or seven, and have each group form a circle.
- Give each group a balloon or beach ball.

Directions

On the "go" signal, students begin to volley the ball or balloon. For the first minute, they may use any body part to move the ball or balloon. If the ball or balloon hits the ground or goes out of the area, a student must pick it up and return it to the circle to begin a new attempt to complete the volley around the circle. After the first minute, call out what body part should be used to contact the ball or balloon (e.g., head, elbow, knee, or hip).

Hints and Modifications

- Have students maintain their circles as well as possible. Allow them to move one or two steps back.

• If groups are having problems with too many members trying to hit the ball or balloon at once, remind them to "call it."

CASCADING BALL RELAY

Overview

This is a cooperative relay involving skill and teamwork.

Equipment

- Two towels or large garbage bags for each team
- One playground or volleyball ball for each team

Preparation

- Divide students into teams of four, and give each group two towels or garbage bags and one ball. Each group divides into two sets of partners. One set of partners holds each towel or garbage bag.
- Have each team form a line on one side of the gym.

Directions

On the "go" signal, each pair of partners picks up its towel or garbage bag. One set of partners puts the ball on their towel or bag, and the others stand in front of them. The first set of partners passes the ball from towel or bag to the other and runs in front of them to receive another pass. This rotation continues until teams reach the opposite side. If they drop the ball, the team goes back four steps and resumes the passing rotations.

Hints and Modifications

Teams may not throw the ball between sets of partners. The ball must be rolled off one towel or bag onto the other.

CHALLENGES FOR TODAY

Overview

These individual and partner challenges involve balance and skill designed to engage and motivate each student. They are a modification of the same activity for primary level students.

Equipment

- None

Preparation

- Have students find a personal space within the boundaries of the facility.
- Remind the students that challenges are simple for some and more difficult for others. Every person should attempt the challenge for the day and work at his own pace for success.

Directions

Have students attempt one or two challenges each day.

- Scooter: Students sit on the floor with feet extended in front and arms held about chin high. To "scoot," students lift their bottoms and move them toward their heels. Then they extend their legs again and repeat the movement.
- Walk-through: From a push-up position and keeping the hands in place, students walk their feet forward until they are standing. They reverse this movement back to the push-up position. (See page 144.)
- Knee jump to standing: From a kneeling position and with heels and buttocks touching and toes pointing back, students jump to a standing position—swinging the arms up and forward in one motion.
- Kick-through: From a push-up position, students bring their right feet under their bodies and touch their left hands. They reverse this using the left leg. Have students try lifting their hand up and balancing it on the opposite hand and foot (see figure in chapter 3, page 49).
- Knee slap and heel tap: From a standing position, students lift their right knees and touch them with their left hands. They repeat this using the left hand to touch the right knee. They can follow this movement by lifting the right heel and touching it, behind the body, with the left hand. Students may repeat this using the left knee and right hand. After doing the four movements, students should slowly increase speed. (See page 144.)
- Double scooter: Students find partners of approximately the same size. Partners sit on the floor facing each other on each other's feet. With arms joined, they scoot forward or backward by cooperating—when one student moves the other lifts with her feet.
- Rising sun: Partners lie face down with heads together and feet in opposite directions. A playground or volleyball is placed between their heads. They attempt to stand and return to their original position without losing control of the ball or touching it with their hands.

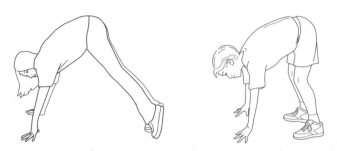

Walk-through: *(a)* Starting position and *(b)* ending position.

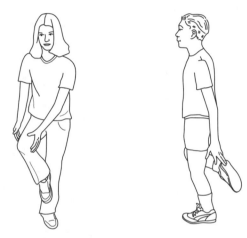

Knee slap and heel tap: *(a)* Starting position and *(b)* ending position.

Hints and Modifications

- Caution students to always be under control and to cooperate with others.
- Remind students that to be successful in balancing, they must perform movements slowly and with control.
- Use your imagination and your students' imaginations to develop challenges that are beneficial to physical development and in which all students have the opportunity to succeed.

Celebrating Student Success

Students expend a great deal of energy and time learning and practicing skills. Just as student athletes at the secondary level learn and practice for games or matches, elementary students are motivated to learn and enhance their skills for a culminating event. In addition to providing students with motivation, the following events provide excellent opportunities to promote and demonstrate the effectiveness of programs to parents and other community members.

Each of the following activities provides examples of culminating events that are reflective of a comprehensive program.

- Skills-R-Us: Skill Development
- Anything Goes: Creativity
- Physical Education Challenge: Individual or Group Challenges

Cumulative Activities

These programs are not designed to be competitive conclusions to an instructional unit or special event. As a part of a developmentally centered physical education program, they must be instructional, inclusive of all students, and fun for everyone.

Preparation is critical to the success of these programs. Before the conclusion of each instructional unit students need to know what activities will be included. In addition, dates must be set for afterschool events well in advance, notices should be placed in school newsletters, and student-written invitations should be sent to families and others students would like to invite.

Early in the preparation volunteers—used for judging and scoring—must be contacted. Older students and high schoool athletes work well in these positions while providing positive role models for younger students.

SKILLS-R-US

Overview

At the conclusion of each unit or periodically during the year, students have the opportunity to practice and demonstrate their newly acquired skills in a fun atmosphere.

Equipment

Equipment varies with skills to be practiced. On the date of each event, arrange equipment in stations. Assign intermediate students to be "buddies" with primary students, working with them at their stations.

Directions

After giving a brief introduction, divide students and guests into groups to begin demonstrating skills and having fun. If parents are present and participating, have them work with their children; the children should demonstrate or teach the parents how to perform each activity. Groups rotate activity stations every 10 minutes or more often, depending on the number of participants.

At the conclusion of the activity period, allow time for students and guests to talk about the activities and to celebrate the knowledge and skills gained during the unit.

Sample Primary Stations for Volleyball

1. Beach ball toss and hit: In groups of three, students stand approximately 4 feet (1.2 meters) away from their "buddies." To begin, one buddy stands inside a hula hoop and tosses the ball to one player, who hits it back. The buddy must be able to catch the ball without leaving the hula hoop. After catching, or attempting

to catch, the ball, players rotate; the catcher goes to the end of the line, the tosser becomes the catcher.

2. Hit and run: In groups of three, players form lines facing another group of three approximately four feet (1.2 meters) away. Give one beach ball to each pair of groups. The person with the ball tosses it across to the first player in the group facing his group. After tossing, the player runs to the end of the line. The player receiving the ball hits it back and runs to the end of their line. The rotation continues for two minutes. After the students are successful at tossing the ball, try having one line toss and the other setting it back. In this variation, one line always tosses and the other sets. Therefore, students switch lines after each toss and set.

3. Not on my side: This is a variation of the standard "clean up the backyard." Arrange a four-area court—similar to a Four Square court—with each area approximately 15 feet × 15 feet (4.5 meters × 4.5 meters). You can use a net or plastic tape to mark a court, and the net should be approximately 6 feet (1.8 meters) off the ground. To begin, assign four students to each area, and give each one a ball. Place an additional ball on the ground in each area. On the "go" signal, players begin tossing the ball into other courts. If a ball lands outside a court, the person tossing it must retrieve it. After two minutes, stop play, count the number of balls in each area, and award points. The group with the fewest balls in its court wins. In a variation, players toss the ball up to themselves and set it over the net or tape.

Sample Intermediate Stations

1. Partner pass: Have partners stand 5 feet (1.5 meters) apart, with one partner tossing the ball for either a set or bump and the receiving partner returning the toss. Partners should progress from tossing, returning, and catching to volleying back and forth.

2. Boo-boo: Divide the students into two groups, each forming a line on the side of the court. Six players from either end enter the court; three go to each side of the net. To begin, someone tosses the ball to one side. The players on that side return it over the net to the other side. The volley continues until a team makes a mistake. The side that makes the mistake quickly runs off the court and is replaced by the next three players in line.

3. Shuffle: Players line up along the side and end lines of a volleyball court. Assign four players to the center, each with a ball.

On the "go" signal, line players take a ready position and begin to shuffle in the direction announced. The center players count out loud to 15 and then toss the ball to a line player, who must return it to the center player. If successful, the line player replaces the center player.

4. Pass, set, and over: Divide students into groups of five. Have the players form lines at the end of a court. Each group has a ball. Players assume three court positions: passer, setter, and spiker. One player goes to the opposite side of the court and is the "catcher," while the fifth player keeps the ball and stands by the passer. To begin, the player with the ball tosses it to the passer, who passes to the setter, who in turn sets the ball to the spiker, who hits the ball over the net. The catcher retrieves the ball and moves to the fifth position, and all others move up one position. Award a point for each successful rotation of pass, set, and over.

5. Basketball set: Divide students into groups equaling the number of available baskets. The first three players from each group stand in positions near the basket, with one player holding the ball. To begin, the ball is tossed to one player, who sets it to the third, who attempts to set the ball into the basket. Award one point for each basket made.

Hints and Modifications

- Allow individual students or small groups to decide activities. The students should present each new activity to the audience.
- Place illustrations and written information around the room.

ANYTHING GOES

Overview

This event allows students to use their creativity to design activity challenges reflecting those presented in class.

Equipment

This is determined by the activities.

Preparation

Students plan and organize this event. To create the general activity, students should have sufficient time to discuss and plan as well as develop some general guidelines related to safety and appropriate activities. For more preparation notes, see the next section.

Directions

Students enjoy becoming involved in the planning and organizing of special events. Planning the event involves organizing by grade levels, classes, or multiage groups. Grouping should be decided three to four weeks before the event. Each group has the opportunity to develop one activity. They must decide on how it is to be organized, conducted, and scored. The group developing the activity is in charge of procuring and arranging all equipment, setting up the activity, and explaining it to all involved. After this process is completed for all activities, have a pamphlet listing all the activities printed and distributed to all participating groups. In addition, send notices to parents, district staff, and community members. During physical education classes or at other prearranged times, students should have the opportunity to practice activities and organize the event.

Sample Activities

As designed by students at LP Brown Elementary, Olympia, Washington.

Great Peanut Race

Equipment

- Two buckets
- Large bag of peanuts for each team
- One plastic spoon for each team
- Four cone markers for each team

In teams of four to six, students line up behind a bucket of peanuts. Give each team one plastic spoon. On the "go" signal, the first player picks up a peanut, places it on her spoon and runs a zigzag course between cones to the finish line, approximately 15 yards (13.5 meters) away. At the finish line, she places the peanut in an empty bucket, runs back through the zigzag, and hands the spoon to the next teammate. The relay continues for three minutes or until one team gets all its peanuts in the finish line bucket.

Tube It Relay

Equipment

- Two large inner tubes
- Six cone markers for each group

Students are divided into groups of six. A course is set with two end lines 25 yards (7.5 meters) apart with cones placed at the start and end lines as well as a set 10 yards (6 meters) from the start line. Two inner tubes are set at the start line. Each team lines up behind the tubes at the start line. On the "go" signal, the first two players from each team pick up an inner tube and roll it to the end line. When they reach the end line, they stand back-to-back and place the inner tubes over their heads (the tubes should reach their waists and stay there). With the tubes in place, the pair begins to move toward the start line. When they reach the 10-yard (6-meter) line, they are met by two teammates and then lie down. The "tube people" are then rolled to the start line. After reaching the start line, the "rollers" take the tubes and begin the sequence again. The race continues for five minutes. Team points are awarded for each complete run.

Bombs Away

Equipment

- One 6-foot to 8-foot (1.8-meter to 2.4-meter) step ladder
- Blindfold
- Large bucket
- Twenty water balloons
- Two cone markers for each team

Students are divided into groups of six. One team member, the balloon handler, is placed on the ladder and is blindfolded. A teammate is assigned to the balloon handler, and the remaining teammates are carriers. Cones are placed 20 feet (6 meters) apart in front of the ladder.

On the "go" signal, two players hold their team's bucket and begin moving from one cone to the other without stopping or changing pace. When they reach the ladder, the blindfolded player is handed a balloon and attempts to drop it into the bucket. After catching a balloon the partners run to the start line, place the balloon on the ground and give the bucket to the next pair, who move the ladder. The rotation continues for 5 minutes. After 5 minutes, balloons are counted.

Where Did It Go?

Equipment

- Five Frisbees
- Two cones
- One blindfold
- A playing area of concentric circles 10, 15, 20, 25, and 40 feet (3, 4.5, 6, 7.5, and 12 meters) in diameter, with a throwing line 5 feet (1.5 meters) from the outside circle.

Divide students into groups of six. Each team is lined up behind the throwing cone. The first player is blindfolded, the second becomes the retriever, and the third hands Frisbees to the thrower.

On the "go" signal, the thrower begins to throw toward the circles. Points are awarded as follows: inner circle, eight points; six for the next circle; five for the next; then four; and three for the outer circle. After five throws, players rotate from hander to thrower, thrower to retriever, and retriever to the end of the line.

Hints and Modifications

Be sure to evaluate each activity on the basis of safety.

PHYSICAL EDUCATION CHALLENGE

Overview

This annual event is designed as a culmination and celebration of the year's physical education programs. Each activity included has been taught and practiced during the school year.

Equipment

This depends on activities that students present.

Directions

After giving a brief introduction, divide students and guests into groups to begin demonstrating skills and having fun. If parents are present and participating, have them work with their children; the children should demonstrate or teach the parents how to perform each activity. Groups rotate activity stations every 10 minutes or more often, depending on the number of participants.

Sample Activities

Accuracy Throw

Equipment

- One hula hoop
- One poly spot
- Cone markers for throwing line
- Four tennis balls

Volunteers

- One scorer
- Two ball retrievers

Students throw at a target 50 feet (15 meters) away. Each student gets four attempts using a tennis ball. The target is a 36-inch (.9-meter) hula hoop suspended 3 feet (.9 meter) from the ground. A poly spot is placed in the center of the hoop. Each hit made inside the hoop will be recorded as one point. If the center spot is hit, an additional two bonus points will be awarded.

Volleyball Accuracy Set

Equipment

- One set of stands and volleyball net
- Ten volleyballs
- Volleyball cart or cones to mark target area

Volunteers

- One scorer
- One or two ball retrievers

Students standing five feet from a net set toss balls over a 6-foot (1.8-meter) net into a 2-foot × 2-foot (.6-meter × .6-meter) target. The target is placed 10 feet (3 meters) away from the net. Each student has 10 attempts. Record the number landing in the target.

Basketball Shootout

Equipment

- Five basketballs
- Five poly spots or cones

Volunteers

- One scorer
- Two ball retrievers
- One ball passer (receives retrieved balls and passes to the shooter)

Each student has 60 seconds to make as many baskets as possible from five specific shot positions. Students start on the right side of the basketball hoop and continue clockwise to each spot. Appoint a student to be a rebounder and another to record the total number of shots made.

Speed Rope Skipping

Equipment

- One rope for each person jumping. Have several different sizes available.

Volunteers

- One scorer
- One timer

Students jump for 30 seconds. Determine scores with the number of times the rope successfully goes under the feet, and award one point for each successful jump.

Push-Ups

Equipment

• None

Volunteer

• One scorer

Students perform push-ups to a three-second cadence. To be counted as a full push-up, arms must be bent to a 90-degree angle at the elbow in the down position and the chest must touch a Nerf football placed directly under the sternum. Give two warnings for not completing a push-up: e.g., bending the arms, not touching the ball, or going off cadence. Warnings are cumulative. The attempt is over on the third mistake.

Team Bowling

Equipment

• Bowling lanes (pins and ball)

Volunteers

• One scorer for each lane

Students compete in teams of two. Each bowler completes five frames. Bowler 1 bowls frames 1, 3, 5, 7, and 9; and bowler 2 bowls frames 2, 4, 6, 8, and 10. When bowler 1 takes her turn, the other team member returns the ball and removes the downed pins. After the frame is completed, reset the pins and bowler 2 takes his turn. The total number of pins knocked down determines the team score. No bonus points are awarded for spares or strikes.

Obstacle Course

Equipment

• Five hula hoops
• Three poly spots
• Two hurdles
• Two stands
• One crash mat
• Plastic tape
• Three cone markers

Volunteers

- One timer
- One starter
- One observer
- One course maintenance person

Students participate in this event as members of a three-person team and as individuals. Record and add individual times to determine a team score. Students have one attempt to run the course. If they fail to clear an object or make a mistake, the observer adds a one-second penalty per mistake to their time.

Students begin by jumping through hoops set in a hopscotch pattern; then they jump onto three poly spots set 2 feet (.6 meter) apart, over two hurdles—5 feet (1.5 meters) apart, under a bar (plastic tape) set between two standards 26 inches (66 centimeters) in the air (put a crash mat on the floor)—zigzag through three cone markers set 3 feet (.9 meter) apart, and sprint to the finish line.

1. Start
2. Hoop jump
3. Poly spot jump
4. Hurdles
5. Under 26–inch bar
6. Zigzag
7. Sprint
8. Finish

Class or School Spirit Award

Equipment

- One award plaque or certificate

Volunteers

- Three of the volunteers working the event

This special award is presented to the class or school whose students demonstrate exceptional cooperation; spirit; teamwork; and respect for teammates, other participants, and volunteers (e.g., cheering for the members and those from other classes or schools, being in the appropriate place at the proper time, and respecting volunteers).

Hints and Modifications

- Use community members, school board members, principals, and other staff to serve as officials.
- Create a poster of all the top-achieving students to post in each building.

References

American Medical Association. August 2002. *Richard Strauss MD Report on National Longitudinal Survey of Youth.* Chicago, IL: Author.

Centers for Disease Control and Prevention. August 2002. *Report on Children's Health.* Atlanta, GA: Author.

National Association for Sport and Physical Education. 1995. *Moving Into the Future: National Standards for Physical Education: A Guide to Content and Assessment.* St. Louis: Mosby.

Poppen, J. 1990. *The Best of Games That Come Alive.* Puyallup, WA: Action Productions.

Rankin, K. 1989. *Physical Education Guidelines for School Administrators.* Olympia, WA: OSPI.

U.S. Department of Health and Human Services. November 2000. *Healthy people 2010.* Washington, DC: Author.

About the Author

Jeff Carpenter, MS, is the former chair of the American Alliance for Health, Physical Education, Recreation and Dance (AAHPERD) Physical Best committee and is a Physical Best national expert and trainer. He has 30 years of teaching and administrative experience in physical education in grades K–12, and he has authored three previous books on K–12 physical education programs and activities. Carpenter has presented activity sessions at 14 national AAHPERD conventions; at numerous state and regional physical education conferences; and at conferences and conventions for the Association for Supervision and Curriculum Development (ASCD), the Parent Teacher Student Association (PTSA), the Governor's Council on Physical Fitness

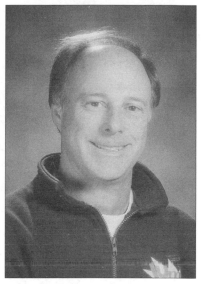

and Sport, and the President's Council on Physical Fitness and Sport.

As the former state supervisor for health and physical education for the state of Washington, Carpenter was responsible for developing statewide curriculum guidelines and outcomes. He has also consulted with more than 40 school districts across the nation on the development and implementation of success-oriented and student-centered physical education programs. Additionally, he has been an adjunct professor at six different universities, teaching both undergraduate and graduate classes in physical education activities, theory, and philosophy.

Carpenter has received numerous awards and honors, including the National Association for Sport and Physical Education Channing Mann Award for the physical education administrator of the year (2002), the AAHPERD Honor Award for K–12 physical education (1997), the AAHPERD/American Heart Association (AHA) Jump Rope for Heart National Honor Award (1997), and the President's Council on Physical Fitness and Sport Commendation (1987). He is a member of AAHPERD and a former president of the Washington Alliance for Health, Physical Education, Recreation and Dance and is a former chair of the AAHPERD/AHA Jump Rope for Heart Committee. He is currently the director of health, fitness, and athletic programs—health and intervention services for the Olympia School District in Olympia, Washington, where he resides. In his free time, he enjoys playing golf, skiing, and boating.